ENDURING WISDOM

Timeless Lessons on Perseverance and Inner Strength

FELIX GRAYSON

MINDSPARK
PUBLISHING

To those who rise after every fall, who find strength in struggle, and who inspire others to do the same—this book is for you. May your journey be one of courage, resilience, and enduring purpose.

"The human spirit is stronger than anything that can happen to it."

— *C.C. Scott*

ABOUT STONED PHILOSOPHER

Welcome to the *Stoned Philosopher* series—where timeless wisdom meets the modern world.

Each book distills powerful lessons from history's greatest minds, leaders, and thinkers—transforming their ideas into practical insights for today's challenges.

From mastering habits, calm, and resilience to understanding success, leadership, and meaning, this collection invites you to think deeper, live wiser, and see life from new perspectives.

Whether you're exploring *Modern Zen*, uncovering *The Wisdom of Warriors*, or seeking clarity through *The Art of Perspective*, every title offers a journey toward self-mastery and understanding.

Discover the full *Stoned Philosopher* collection and more at **FelixGrayson.com**, home of **Mind-Spark Publishing**—where knowledge, philosophy, and storytelling come together to spark lifelong curiosity.

Wisdom isn't something we find—it's something we grow into.

Let the journey begin.

CONTENTS

INTRODUCTION: A JOURNEY TO ENDURING STRENGTH

Resilience. Inner strength. Purpose. These are words we often hear, yet they can feel elusive when we face life's complexities. How do we remain steadfast when the ground beneath us shifts? How do we cultivate strength in moments of doubt or adversity? And how do we uncover meaning in the chaos of life's challenges?

This book was born from these questions. It is an exploration of the timeless principles that have guided humanity through hardship and toward growth. It is a celebration of the enduring spirit that resides within each of us—a spirit capable of withstanding life's storms and emerging stronger, wiser, and more purposeful.

As you hold this book in your hands, you are about to embark on a journey. It is a journey that will traverse the lessons of history, the wisdom of philosophy, and the insights of modern science. Together, we will uncover the tools to navigate life's challenges, build inner fortitude, and live with purpose. But this is not just a journey of discovery—it is a journey of transformation.

The Call to Resilience

Life is not a straight path. It twists and turns, often without warning. The plans we make may falter, the certainties we cling to may dissolve, and the challenges we never anticipated may come to define us. Yet within this uncertainty lies an invitation: the call to resilience.

Resilience is not about denying pain or pretending challenges do not exist. It is about learning to rise. It is the quiet strength that allows us to endure, adapt, and grow. It is the ability to face life's trials with courage, find meaning in the struggle, and transform adversity into a stepping stone for growth.

This book is a response to that call. It offers a roadmap for building resilience—not as a fixed trait but as an ongoing practice. Through the lessons shared within these pages, you will discover that resilience is not reserved for the extraordinary. It is available to all of us, in the choices we make, the values we uphold, and the perspectives we embrace.

The Power Within

Resilience begins within. It is rooted in the strength of the human spirit—the capacity to persevere, to create meaning, and to act with integrity even in the face of uncertainty. But inner strength is not an innate gift; it is cultivated over time, through self-awareness, intentional practice, and alignment with our values.

This book will guide you in uncovering your own inner strength. You will learn how to identify the values that anchor you, the purpose that inspires you, and the mindset that empowers you to navigate life's challenges. Through stories of historical figures, philosophical reflections, and practical exercises, you will gain the tools to cultivate a resilience that is uniquely your own.

The Lessons of History

To understand resilience, we must look to those

who have walked this path before us. History is rich with examples of individuals who have demonstrated extraordinary resilience and inner strength. From Nelson Mandela's unwavering commitment to justice to Viktor Frankl's search for meaning in the depths of suffering, these stories remind us of what is possible when we embrace life's challenges with courage and purpose.

But resilience is not confined to individual stories. It is also found in the collective strength of communities, movements, and cultures. From the unity of the Underground Railroad to the perseverance of societies rebuilding after war, history reveals the power of connection and shared purpose in fostering resilience.

As we explore these lessons, you will see that resilience is not about being unshaken by life's trials. It is about rising to meet them, again and again, with a spirit of determination and hope.

A Practical Guide

While this book draws on the wisdom of the past, its purpose is rooted in the present. It is designed to equip you with practical tools and in-sights that you can apply in your own life. Each chapter offers actionable guidance on building resilience, cultivating inner strength, and living with purpose.

These principles are not meant to be theoretical. They are meant to be lived. Whether you are navigating personal challenges, striving toward a goal, or seeking greater meaning in your daily life, the lessons in this book will empower you to move forward with confidence and clarity.

Why This Matters Now

We live in a world that is both interconnected and unpredictable. The pace of change is fast-er than ever, and the challenges we face—in-dividually and collectively—are complex and multifaceted. In such a world, resilience is not a luxury; it is a necessity.

This book is not just a guide to surviving; it is a guide to thriving. It is an invitation to cultivate the strength and purpose needed to navigate life's uncertainties and contribute meaningfully to the world around you. It is a call to embrace the enduring spirit within yourself and to inspire it in others.

An Invitation to Transform

As you begin this book, I encourage you to approach it not as a passive reader but as an active participant. Reflect on the lessons, apply the exercises, and consider how these insights can shape your own journey. This is not a one-size-fits-all guide; it is a framework for discovering what resilience means to you.

Imagine the life you want to create. Imagine the strength you want to embody, the purpose you want to pursue, and the legacy you want to leave. This book is your companion on that journey, offering the tools and inspiration to help you turn those aspirations into reality.

A Journey Worth Taking

Resilience is not about avoiding challenges—it is about embracing them. It is about finding strength in the struggle, meaning in the uncertainty, and purpose in the journey. It is about rising, again and again, with the knowledge that each step forward brings us closer to the person we are meant to be.

As you turn the pages of this book, may you find not only guidance but also inspiration. May you discover the wisdom within yourself, the strength to persevere, and the courage to live a life filled with purpose and meaning.

This is your journey. It begins now. Let us walk it together.

CHAPTER 1: THE ROOTS OF RESILIENCE – UNDERSTANDING TRUE STRENGTH

The Evolution of Resilience

Resilience, as a concept and a trait, has been intricately woven into the fabric of human existence. It is a testament to our ability not only to endure hardship but to adapt, innovate, and thrive in the face of adversity. From the earliest days of humankind, when survival depended on withstanding harsh environments and unpredictable threats, to the complex challenges of modern life, resilience has remained a cornerstone of progress. Understanding its evolution helps illuminate how this quality has defined humanity's trajectory and how it continues to shape our individual and collective lives.

The Origins of Resilience: Survival Against All Odds

In the harsh landscapes of prehistory, resilience was not an abstract virtue; it was a matter of survival. Early humans faced relentless challenges—unforgiving climates, scarcity of resources, and the ever-present threat of predators. In this primal world, the capacity to adapt was essential. Those who could endure prolonged periods of scarcity, recover from injuries, and adapt to shifting environments were more likely to survive and pass on their genes.

Archaeological evidence paints a vivid picture of resilience in early human communities. The ability to create tools, harness fire, and eventually cultivate food demonstrates not only ingenuity but also an enduring spirit of perseverance. Consider the migration of early humans out of Africa some 70,000 years ago—a monumental feat of resilience. These migrations required extraordinary determination, as small bands of humans traversed vast, inhospitable terrains in search of sustenance and safety. Their success laid the groundwork for human expansion across the globe.

Historical Examples of Resilience in Action

As civilizations emerged, resilience took on new dimensions. It was no longer solely about physical survival but also about the endurance of ideas, cultures, and values in the face of adversity. History offers countless examples of individuals and societies that demonstrated remarkable resilience, shaping the world as we know it today.

One compelling example is the story of the Spartans, whose way of life embodied resilience. From a young age, Spartan boys were subjected to rigorous training designed to instill discipline, strength, and an unyielding resolve. This cultivation of resilience was not merely for personal glory; it was essential for defending their city-state in a hostile world. The Spartans' legendary stand at Thermopylae, where a small force held off a vastly superior Persian army, remains a symbol of resilience against overwhelming odds.

On a societal level, the rebuilding of Japan after World War II showcases collective resilience. Emerging from the devastation of war, with cities reduced to rubble and the economy in shambles, the Japanese people undertook a remarkable transformation. Through perseverance, innovation, and a deep commitment to rebuilding, Japan emerged as a global economic power within decades. This rebirth was a testament to the enduring spirit of a nation united by shared purpose.

Resilience as a Cultural and Philosophical

Ideal

Resilience is not only reflected in historical events but also deeply embedded in cultural and philosophical traditions. Many ancient philosophies recognized the importance of resilience and sought to teach its principles.

Stoicism, a school of philosophy originating in ancient Greece, offers profound insights into resilience. Stoics like Epictetus and Marcus Aurelius emphasized the importance of accepting what we cannot control while focusing our efforts on what lies within our power. Their teachings encourage the cultivation of inner strength to endure life's inevitable hardships with grace and dignity. "You have power over your mind—not outside events," wrote Marcus Aurelius in his *Meditations*. "Realize this, and you will find strength."

Eastern philosophies also provide timeless lessons on resilience. In Buddhism, the concept of *dukkha* acknowledges the pervasive nature of suffering, urging practitioners to cultivate mindfulness and equanimity in response. The Taoist principle of *wu wei*—effortless action—

teaches resilience through adaptability, encouraging us to flow with life's changes rather than resist them.

The Modern Face of Resilience

Today, resilience remains as relevant as ever, though its expressions have evolved to meet the demands of contemporary life. The challenges we face are less likely to involve survival against predators or invasions and more likely to center on psychological, social, and economic pressures. Yet, the same core principles that sustained our ancestors apply: adaptability, determination, and a capacity for renewal.

Modern resilience can be seen in the stories of individuals who overcome personal hardships to achieve greatness. Think of figures like Helen Keller, who triumphed over the dual barriers of blindness and deafness to become a celebrated author and advocate, or Malala Yousafzai, who transformed a near-fatal attack into a platform for global education reform. Their stories remind us that resilience is not merely about enduring hardship but using it as a springboard for growth and positive change.

On a collective level, resilience is evident in how communities respond to crises. The global response to the COVID-19 pandemic showcased resilience on multiple fronts—from frontline workers tirelessly battling the virus to individuals adapting to new ways of living and working. It highlighted our capacity to endure, innovate, and collaborate in the face of unprecedented challenges.

Resilience as a Timeless Virtue

The evolution of resilience, from its primal origins to its modern expressions, underscores its timeless relevance. It is a quality that transcends cultures, eras, and circumstances, offering a universal lesson: while we cannot always control the challenges life presents, we can choose how we respond. By drawing inspiration from history and philosophy, we can cultivate resilience in our own lives, transforming hardship into strength and adversity into growth.

This understanding of resilience's evolution sets the stage for deeper exploration in the chapters to come. It invites readers to reflect on their own capacity for endurance and to recognize the profound legacy of resilience that they inherit as members of the human story.

The Philosophy of Inner Strength

Resilience, while often associated with the ability to withstand external pressures, is deeply rooted in the philosophy of inner strength. Across centuries and cultures, thinkers have explored what it means to cultivate an unshakable core—a reserve of strength that enables individuals to endure life's trials with grace, courage, and purpose. Inner strength, as revealed through philosophy, is less about brute endurance and more about a profound understanding of self, the nature of adversity, and the capacity to align with higher principles.

Stoicism: The Art of Endurance

Perhaps no philosophical tradition has contributed more to the understanding of inner strength than Stoicism. Emerging in ancient Greece and later flourishing in Rome, Stoicism teaches that true resilience lies in mastering one's mind and emotions rather than attempting to control external events. At its core is the recognition that while we cannot dictate what happens to us, we retain complete authority over how we respond.

Epictetus, a former slave turned philosopher, exemplifies this principle. Despite enduring immense hardship, he taught that freedom and strength come from within. "Man is disturbed not by things," he wrote, "but by the views he takes of them." This idea, that our perceptions shape our reality, empowers individuals to transcend suffering by reframing their experiences.

Marcus Aurelius, the Roman emperor and a devoted Stoic, expanded on this concept in his *Meditations*. Writing during a time of political unrest and personal loss, he reflected on the importance of focusing on one's own actions and maintaining virtue amidst chaos. "You have power over your mind — not outside events. Realize this, and you will find strength," he advised. For Marcus, inner strength was not merely a philosophical exercise but a practical tool for navigating the burdens of leadership and life.

Stoicism's emphasis on rationality and acceptance offers a blueprint for cultivating inner strength in any era. By recognizing what lies within our control and letting go of what does not, we can free ourselves from the tyranny of external circumstances and build an enduring foundation of resilience.

Eastern Philosophy: Harmony and Balance

While Stoicism emphasizes mastery over one's internal state, Eastern philosophies such as Taoism and Buddhism focus on achieving harmony with the flow of life. These traditions teach that inner strength arises not from resistance but from a deep understanding and acceptance of life's impermanence and interconnectedness.

In Taoism, the principle of *wu wei*, often translated as "effortless action," provides a powerful metaphor for resilience. Rather than forcing one's way through challenges, *wu wei* encourages individuals to align with the natural rhythms of life, much like water flowing around obstacles. This fluidity, Taoists believe, is the essence of strength. As Laozi writes in the *Tao Te Ching*, "The soft overcomes the hard; the weak overcomes the strong." This paradox illustrates how inner strength is often found in adaptability and humility rather than brute force.

Buddhism, on the other hand, offers profound insights into the nature of suffering and the path to liberation. Central to Buddhist philosophy is the concept of *dukkha*, or the inherent unsatisfactoriness of life. Rather than denying or avoiding suffering, Buddhism teaches practitioners to confront it with mindfulness and compassion. By cultivating awareness through practices like meditation, individuals can develop the equanimity needed to face life's challenges without being overwhelmed. The *Eightfold Path*, a set of ethical and mental practices, provides a practical framework for building resilience through clarity, discipline, and right action.

Both Taoism and Buddhism emphasize that inner strength is not a static quality but a dynamic process of growth and self-discovery. By embracing the impermanent and ever-changing nature of life, individuals can find strength in the present moment and respond to adversity with calm and wisdom.

Inner Strength as a Way of Life

While Stoic and Eastern philosophies differ in their approaches, they converge on a critical insight: inner strength is not an innate trait possessed by a select few but a skill that can be cultivated through deliberate practice. This understanding transforms resilience from a passive quality into an active pursuit, encouraging individuals to integrate its principles into their daily lives.

Practices such as journaling, mindfulness, and self-reflection serve as powerful tools for fostering inner strength. Marcus Aurelius' *Meditations* is an enduring example of the power of journaling. Through writing, he clarified his thoughts, reaffirmed his values, and prepared himself for the challenges ahead. Today, this practice remains a valuable method for cultivating self-awareness and resilience.

Mindfulness, rooted in Buddhist traditions, offers another pathway to inner strength. By anchoring attention in the present moment, mindfulness helps individuals break free from cycles of rumination and anxiety, enabling them to

approach life's challenges with greater clarity
and composure. In a world characterized by
constant distractions, mindfulness provides a
refuge—a means of reconnecting with one's
inner self and regaining balance.

Philosophy in Action

The teachings of ancient philosophers are not
relics of the past but living wisdom that continues to inspire resilience in modern times. Consider the example of Viktor Frankl, a Holocaust
survivor and the founder of logotherapy. Drawing on Stoic principles, Frankl maintained that
even in the most dehumanizing circumstances, individuals retain the freedom to choose
their attitude. His seminal work, *Man's Search
for Meaning*, illustrates how a sense of purpose
and inner strength can sustain the human spirit
through unimaginable suffering.

Similarly, the principles of mindfulness have
gained widespread recognition in fields rang-
ing from psychology to corporate leadership.
Practices like meditation and mindful breathing,
once confined to monasteries, are now integral
to stress management programs and workplace

wellness initiatives. These practices demonstrate the timeless relevance of philosophical teachings in cultivating resilience.

By embracing the wisdom of Stoicism, Taoism, and Buddhism, individuals can navigate life's complexities with greater strength and clarity. These traditions offer not only theoretical insights but practical tools for overcoming adversity and thriving in a world that often feels overwhelming.

A Timeless Pursuit

The philosophy of inner strength reveals that resilience is not a finite resource to be depleted but a wellspring to be replenished through intentional practice. Whether drawing on Stoic resolve, Taoist adaptability, or Buddhist mindfulness, individuals have the power to cultivate an enduring core of strength that sustains them through life's inevitable trials.

This exploration of philosophical foundations invites readers to reflect on their own approaches to adversity. How do we respond when life challenges us? Do we resist, adapt, or retreat?

By engaging with these questions, we begin to uncover the depths of our inner strength and lay the groundwork for a life defined not by the absence of hardship but by the presence of courage, purpose, and wisdom.

The Science of Resilience

Resilience is not merely a philosophical ideal or a product of historical necessity—it is deeply rooted in our biology and psychology. Modern scientific research has illuminated the mechanisms that enable individuals to recover from setbacks, adapt to challenges, and even thrive under pressure. By understanding the science of resilience, we can learn how to cultivate it in our own lives, leveraging the remarkable adaptability of the human brain and body to build enduring inner strength.

The Neurobiology of Resilience: The Brain's Adaptability

At the heart of resilience lies the human brain, a dynamic organ with an extraordinary capacity for change. Neuroscientists refer to this ability as neuroplasticity, the brain's capacity to reorganize itself by forming new neural connections. Neuroplasticity allows us to adapt to new circumstances, recover from trauma, and even reshape our responses to stress.

The amygdala, often called the brain's "fear center," plays a critical role in our stress response. When we encounter a threat, the amygdala triggers the release of stress hormones like cortisol and adrenaline, preparing the body for a fight-or-flight response. While this reaction is essential for survival, chronic activation can lead to burnout and emotional exhaustion. Resilient individuals, however, demonstrate a more balanced response. Research shows that they often have stronger connections between the prefrontal cortex, the brain's rational decision-making hub, and the amygdala. This connection allows them to regulate their emotional responses, maintaining calm under pressure.

Moreover, the brain's ability to adapt extends to its emotional circuitry. Studies have shown that practices such as mindfulness meditation can increase gray matter density in regions of the brain associated with emotional regulation and self-awareness. These changes enhance our capacity to cope with adversity, demonstrating that resilience is not fixed but can be actively developed.

The Role of Grit and Determination

While the brain's adaptability provides a biological foundation for resilience, psychological traits like grit and determination are equally essential. Angela Duckworth, a psychologist and researcher, has defined grit as "passion and perseverance for long-term goals." In her groundbreaking research, Duckworth demonstrated that grit, more than talent or intelligence, predicts success across diverse domains, from academic achievement to professional performance.

Grit involves the sustained effort to overcome obstacles and the willingness to persist in the face of failure. Unlike fleeting motivation, which can waver in challenging times, grit is rooted in a deeper sense of purpose and commitment. For example, athletes who endure grueling training regimens or entrepreneurs who persist after multiple business failures often exhibit high levels of grit. Their determination enables them to stay focused on their goals, even when imme-diate results are elusive.

The good news is that grit can be cultivated. Research suggests that fostering a growth mind-set—the belief that abilities and intelligence can be developed through effort—plays a key role in building determination. By viewing challeng-es as opportunities to grow rather than insur-mountable obstacles, individuals can strengthen their resolve and enhance their resilience.

Stress and Resilience: The Science of Adapta-tion

Stress, while often perceived as harmful, can also be a catalyst for growth. Psychologists refer to this phenomenon as "post-traumatic growth," the process by which individuals emerge stron-ger and more capable after experiencing adver-sity. This counterintuitive idea underscores the dual nature of stress: while excessive or chronic stress can be debilitating, manageable levels of stress can build resilience by challenging us to adapt and overcome.

The Yerkes-Dodson Law, a psychological principle, illustrates this balance. It posits that performance improves with moderate levels of stress, as it heightens focus and energy. However, when stress becomes overwhelming, performance declines. Resilient individuals excel at finding the optimal balance, using stress as a motivator without allowing it to become paralyzing.

One of the key factors influencing this balance is the release of oxytocin, often called the "cuddle hormone." While oxytocin is best known for its role in social bonding, it also plays a crucial role in the stress response. During challenging times, oxytocin promotes connection and support-seeking behavior, helping individuals navigate adversity more effectively. This discovery highlights the importance of social relationships in resilience, as we will explore further in later chapters.

Practical Strategies for Building Resilience

Understanding the science of resilience empowers us to take deliberate steps to enhance it in our lives. Physical and mental practices that align with our biological and psychological processes can significantly strengthen our capacity to endure and adapt.

Exercise, for example, has been shown to reduce stress, improve mood, and enhance cognitive function—all of which contribute to resilience. Physical activity increases the production of endorphins, which act as natural mood elevators, and promotes the growth of new neurons in the brain, a process known as neurogenesis. These changes not only improve our immediate ability to cope with stress but also build a stronger foundation for long-term resilience.

Sleep is another critical factor. During sleep, the brain consolidates memories, processes emotions, and repairs cellular damage. Chronic sleep deprivation, on the other hand, impairs emotional regulation and weakens the immune system, making it harder to bounce back from adversity. By prioritizing restorative sleep, we enhance our capacity to face challenges with clarity and strength.

Finally, cultivating positive habits like journaling, gratitude practices, and mindfulness meditation can reinforce resilience. Journaling provides an outlet for processing emotions and reflecting on experiences, while gratitude practices shift focus from what is lacking to what is abundant in life. Mindfulness meditation, as mentioned earlier, strengthens neural pathways associated with emotional regulation, equipping us to respond to stressors with greater composure.

The Science of Hope

Resilience is not solely about enduring hardship—it is also about sustaining hope. Research in positive psychology underscores the importance of hope as a psychological resource that bolsters resilience. Hopeful individuals are more likely to set meaningful goals, persevere through challenges, and maintain a sense of optimism about the future.

One striking study revealed that patients recovering from severe illnesses who maintained a hopeful outlook experienced better outcomes than those who succumbed to despair. This finding highlights the interplay between psychological factors and physical well-being, reinforcing the idea that resilience is a holistic quality that encompasses mind and body.

Resilience: A Dynamic Quality

The science of resilience reveals a dynamic and multifaceted quality that integrates neurobiology, psychology, and behavior. It is not an inherent trait possessed by a fortunate few but a skill that can be cultivated through intentional practices and a deeper understanding of how our minds and bodies respond to stress.

As we continue this exploration of resilience, the insights from scientific research provide a foundation for practical application. By harnessing the adaptability of the brain, embracing the principles of grit, and leveraging the power of stress for growth, we can build a reservoir of strength to navigate life's challenges. The journey of resilience is not static but ever-evolving—a testament to the remarkable capacity of human beings to endure, adapt, and thrive.

Recognizing Your Own Resilience

Resilience is often seen as an extraordinary quality, possessed by heroic figures who face immense challenges with unwavering courage.

But the truth is far simpler—and more empowering. Resilience is a trait we all possess, even if we don't always recognize it. The ability to endure hardship, adapt to change, and grow stronger in the face of adversity is as natural to us as breathing. By learning to identify and cultivate our own resilience, we can transform it from a latent capacity into a defining strength.

Understanding Your Resilience Story

Each of us has faced moments that tested our limits, whether they were personal, professional, or emotional. These experiences, though often painful at the time, are the building blocks of resilience. By reflecting on these moments, we can uncover patterns of strength and adaptability that might otherwise go unnoticed.

Consider the story of Malala Yousafzai, who faced unimaginable adversity as a young girl advocating for education in Pakistan. After surviving a near-fatal attack, she channeled her experience into a global movement for girls' education, demonstrating extraordinary resilience. While her story is remarkable, it also serves as a reminder that resilience begins with smaller acts of courage and determination—standing up for one's beliefs, facing daily challenges, or simply moving forward after a setback.

Take a moment to reflect on your own life. What challenges have you overcome? How did you navigate them? Perhaps you endured a difficult job transition, cared for a loved one during an illness, or managed to stay hopeful during uncertain times. These moments, however ordinary they may seem, are powerful indicators of your resilience. Recognizing and valuing them is the first step in strengthening your ability to face future challenges.

Resilience in Practice: Building Self-Awareness

Resilience is closely tied to self-awareness. The more you understand your thoughts, emotions, and behaviors, the better equipped you are to navigate adversity. Psychologists often describe self-awareness as the foundation of emotional intelligence, a key component of resilience.

One practical way to cultivate self-awareness is through journaling. By writing about your experiences, thoughts, and feelings, you create a space for reflection and insight. Marcus Aurelius, the Stoic emperor, used this practice to strengthen his inner resolve. His writings, later published as *Meditations*, reveal a profound understanding of his own mind and the principles that guided his actions. Journaling can serve a similar purpose in your life, helping you identify patterns of strength and areas for growth.

Mindfulness meditation is another powerful tool for building self-awareness. By focusing on the present moment without judgment, mindfulness helps you become more attuned to your inner world. This practice not only reduces stress but also enhances your ability to respond thoughtfully to challenges, rather than reacting impulsively. Over time, mindfulness strengthens the mental "muscles" that support resilience.

Identifying Growth Areas

While everyone possesses resilience, there is always room to grow. Recognizing areas where your resilience can be strengthened is not a sign of weakness but of courage and commitment to self-improvement. Begin by asking yourself the following questions:

- How do I typically respond to setbacks?

- Do I view challenges as opportunities for growth or as insurmountable obstacles?

- How well do I manage stress and regulate my emotions during difficult times?

- Am I able to maintain a sense of purpose and direction in the face of uncertainty?

Your answers to these questions can provide valuable insights into your resilience. For example, if you find that you often become overwhelmed by stress, it may be helpful to explore techniques for stress management, such as exercise, deep breathing, or time management strategies. If you struggle to maintain optimism during tough times, practicing gratitude or reframing negative thoughts could be transformative.

The Role of Self-Compassion

One of the most overlooked aspects of resilience is self-compassion. Many people believe that resilience requires stoic endurance and an unyielding spirit. While determination is important, resilience also depends on the ability to treat oneself with kindness and understanding, especially in moments of failure or vulnerability.

Dr. Kristin Neff, a leading researcher on self-compassion, has found that individuals who practice self-compassion are more resilient in the face of adversity. Self-compassion involves three key elements: self-kindness, recognizing the shared human experience, and mindfulness. Instead of harshly criticizing yourself for perceived shortcomings, try to approach them with the same empathy and support you would offer a friend. This shift in perspective not only reduces emotional distress but also fosters a sense of inner strength and balance.

Practical Exercises for Cultivating Resilience

To deepen your resilience, consider incorporating the following practices into your daily life:

- **The Gratitude Practice**: Each day, take a few

minutes to reflect on three things you are grateful for. Gratitude shifts your focus from what is lacking to what is abundant, reinforcing a positive and resilient mindset.

- **The Resilience Timeline**: Create a timeline of your life, highlighting key challenges you have faced and how you overcame them. Reflect on the strengths, skills, and support systems that helped you navigate those moments. This exercise can provide a powerful reminder of your inner strength and capacity for growth.

- **Visualization for Strength**: Spend a few minutes each day visualizing yourself successfully navigating a future challenge. Imagine the steps you would take, the emotions you would feel, and the resources you would draw upon. Visualization can help reinforce a sense of control and readiness.

A Lifelong Journey

Resilience is not a destination but a journey—a dynamic process of growth and adaptation. It is a quality that evolves with experience, reflection, and intentional practice. By recognizing and valuing your existing resilience, you lay the foundation for continued development. By addressing areas for growth, you expand your capacity to face life's challenges with courage and confidence.

As we conclude this chapter, let us remember that resilience is not an extraordinary gift reserved for a select few. It is a universal human trait, forged in the trials of life and refined through practice. By embracing the tools and insights shared here, you can awaken the resilience within you, transforming it into a wellspring of strength and possibility for the journey ahead.

CHAPTER 2: TESTED BY TIME – LESSONS FROM ADVERSITY

The Transformative Power of Struggle

Adversity has long been regarded as an unwelcome companion, an inevitable force to be
avoided or endured. Yet history, philosophy,
and human experience reveal a different perspective: struggle is not merely something to
survive—it is a crucible that forges strength,
shapes character, and transforms lives. Adversity challenges us to rise above our circumstances, discover inner reservoirs of resilience, and
emerge stronger than before.

Struggle as a Catalyst for Growth

The transformative power of struggle is evident
throughout history. One of the most compelling
examples is Abraham Lincoln, a man whose
life was marked by profound hardship. Born
into poverty, Lincoln endured the death of his
mother at a young age, the loss of several children, and numerous political defeats. Yet, these
struggles did not define him; they refined him.
Lincoln's ability to persevere through personal
and professional trials instilled in him the empathy, resolve, and moral clarity that would later
guide his leadership during one of America's

darkest periods—the Civil War. His struggles were not a hindrance to greatness but the very foundation of it.

Similarly, consider the life of Helen Keller, who lost her sight and hearing at just 19 months old. The magnitude of her adversity was almost unimaginable, yet with the guidance of her teacher, Anne Sullivan, Keller transformed her limitations into a source of profound strength. Her eventual achievements—as an author, activist, and advocate for the disabled—are a testament to the resilience that struggle can inspire. Reflecting on her life, Keller famously remarked, "Character cannot be developed in ease and quiet. Only through experience of trial and suffering can the soul be strengthened, ambition inspired, and success achieved."

These stories remind us that struggle, while painful in the moment, can act as a catalyst for extraordinary growth. It forces us to confront our limitations, adapt to our circumstances, and develop qualities such as perseverance, courage, and empathy that might otherwise remain dormant.

Philosophical Reflections on Adversity

Philosophers across cultures have long acknowledged the transformative potential of adversity. The Stoics, for example, regarded hardship as a necessary ingredient for personal growth. Seneca, a Roman statesman and philosopher, wrote extensively about the benefits of struggle. In his essay *On Providence*, he argued that challenges are a gift from the gods, designed to test and strengthen virtuous individuals. "Difficulties strengthen the mind," Seneca wrote, "as labor does the body."

This perspective is echoed in Eastern philosophy as well. The Buddhist concept of *dukkha*, often translated as suffering or dissatisfaction, is seen not as an obstacle but as a central aspect of life. Rather than fleeing from it, Buddhism teaches practitioners to embrace suffering as an opportunity for growth and enlightenment. Through mindfulness and compassion, individuals can transform pain into wisdom, breaking free from the cycles of fear and despair that adversity often engenders.

These philosophies remind us that while we

cannot always control the presence of struggle in our lives, we can choose how we respond to it. By adopting a mindset that views adversity as a teacher rather than an enemy, we open ourselves to the transformative lessons it has to offer.

The Alchemy of Adversity

The notion that struggle transforms us is not merely philosophical or anecdotal; it is supported by modern psychology. Researchers studying post-traumatic growth have found that individuals who experience significant adversity often report positive changes in their lives afterward. These changes include a deeper appreciation for life, stronger relationships, a heightened sense of personal strength, and a clearer understanding of their priorities and purpose.

One of the most remarkable examples of this phenomenon comes from Viktor Frankl, a Holocaust survivor and the author of *Man's Search for Meaning*. Frankl endured the horrors of Auschwitz, where he lost his wife, parents, and countless friends. Despite this unimaginable suffering, he emerged from the experience with a profound understanding of the human capacity for resilience. Frankl's philosophy, rooted in his experiences, emphasizes the importance of finding meaning in life, even in the face of suffering. "When we are no longer able to change a situation," he wrote, "we are challenged to change ourselves."

Frankl's ability to transform his suffering into a source of insight and purpose illustrates the alchemical power of adversity. Rather than allowing hardship to consume him, he used it as a means to deepen his understanding of life and humanity, ultimately creating a legacy that has inspired millions.

Turning Struggle into Strength

The transformative power of struggle is not reserved for historical figures or philosophers—it is available to all of us. However, tapping into this power requires a conscious effort to reframe our relationship with adversity. Instead of viewing challenges as insurmountable obstacles, we can begin to see them as opportunities for growth.

One way to cultivate this mindset is through the practice of reframing. Reframing involves looking at a situation from a new perspective, focusing on what can be learned or gained rather than what has been lost. For example, losing a job may initially feel like a devastating setback, but it can also be an opportunity to pursue a more fulfilling career path or develop new skills. By shifting our focus from loss to potential, we transform struggle into strength.

Another essential component of turning struggle into strength is perseverance. Challenges often test our endurance, requiring us to push beyond our perceived limits. This process can be uncomfortable, but it is also where growth occurs. Much like a muscle grows stronger through resistance, our character is strengthened through persistence in the face of adversity.

Finally, community plays a crucial role in helping us navigate and learn from struggle. Sharing our experiences with others not only provides emotional support but also fosters a sense of connection and shared humanity. Through these connections, we gain the strength to persevere and the insight to grow.

The Legacy of Struggle

As we reflect on the transformative power of struggle, it becomes clear that adversity is not an impediment to success but an integral part of it. The stories of individuals like Lincoln, Keller, and Frankl demonstrate that greatness is not born of ease but of endurance. Their lives remind us that struggle, while painful, can lead to profound growth and self-discovery.

In our own lives, we may not face challenges of such monumental scale, but the lessons remain the same. Every setback, every failure, and every hardship has the potential to shape us into stronger, wiser, and more compassionate individuals. By embracing struggle as a natural and necessary part of life, we unlock its transformative power, turning adversity into an enduring source of strength and resilience.

Finding Meaning in Hardship

When adversity strikes, it often leaves us grappling with questions that seem unanswerable: Why is this happening? How can I endure this pain? What does it mean for my life? The search for meaning in hardship is a deeply human experience, and it is one that has shaped individuals and civilizations throughout history. At its core, finding meaning transforms suffering from an overwhelming burden into a source of purpose and resilience.

Viktor Frankl and the Search for Meaning

Few have articulated the importance of meaning in hardship as powerfully as Viktor Frankl. A psychiatrist and Holocaust survivor, Frankl endured the horrors of Auschwitz, where he lost his wife, parents, and nearly every semblance of his former life. Yet, in the depths of suffering, he discovered an extraordinary insight: meaning is not something that circumstances grant or deny—it is something we create.

In his seminal work, *Man's Search for Meaning*, Frankl recounts how his ability to endure the unthinkable was rooted in his belief that life, even in the most harrowing conditions, could hold purpose. He observed that those who survived the camps were often those who had something to live for—a goal to achieve, a loved one to reunite with, or a responsibility to fulfill. For Frankl, meaning was the cornerstone of resilience. "Those who have a 'why' to live," he wrote, "can bear almost any 'how.'"

Frankl's experiences led him to develop logotherapy, a psychological framework that emphasizes the pursuit of meaning as the primary driver of human behavior. Central to logotherapy is the idea that meaning can be found in three key ways: through work or achievement, through love or connection, and through the attitude one takes toward unavoidable suffering. This philosophy offers a powerful tool for transforming hardship into an opportunity for growth and purpose.

The Role of Perspective in Finding Meaning

Perspective plays a critical role in the search for meaning. When faced with adversity, our initial instinct is often to focus on what has been lost. While this reaction is natural, it can trap us in a cycle of despair. Meaning arises when we shift our perspective, asking not, "Why did this happen to me?" but, "What can I learn from this?" or "How can I use this experience to grow?"

Consider the story of Malala Yousafzai, who was shot by the Taliban for advocating for girls' education. Rather than allowing this traumatic event to silence her, she reframed it as a call to action. Her suffering became a platform for her advocacy, transforming personal pain into global impact. Malala's ability to find meaning in her hardship illustrates the profound power of perspective in overcoming adversity.

Philosophical traditions also emphasize the importance of reframing hardship. In Buddhism, suffering is viewed not as an aberration but as an integral part of life. The concept of *dukkha* teaches that while pain is inevitable, our relationship to it determines its impact. By approaching suffering with mindfulness and curiosity, we can uncover its deeper lessons and integrate them into our lives. This shift in perspective—seeing adversity as a teacher rather than an enemy—can open the door to profound transformation.

Practical Pathways to Meaning

Finding meaning in hardship is not an abstract ideal; it is a practice that can be cultivated through intentional action and reflection. One practical pathway is through connection. When we face challenges, reaching out to others can provide not only emotional support but also a sense of purpose. By sharing our experiences and offering compassion, we strengthen the bonds that sustain us and discover meaning in our relationships.

Another pathway is through creativity and contribution. Many of history's greatest works of art, literature, and innovation were born from struggle. Frida Kahlo, for example, channeled her physical pain and emotional turmoil into paintings that continue to resonate with audiences worldwide. Her art was not only an expression of her suffering but also a testament to her resilience. Similarly, individuals who contribute to their communities or pursue meaningful projects often find that their efforts bring clarity and purpose to their lives.

Reflection is also a powerful tool for uncovering meaning. Journaling, meditation, or simply taking time to contemplate our experiences can help us identify patterns and insights that might otherwise remain hidden. By asking questions like, "What has this taught me about myself?" or "How can I use this experience to help others?" we transform hardship into a source of wisdom and strength.

The Universality of Meaning

While the paths to meaning may vary, the search itself is universal. Across cultures and traditions, the human spirit has sought to make sense of suffering and to find purpose in the face of adversity. In African philosophy, the concept of *ubuntu*—often translated as "I am because we are"—emphasizes the interconnectedness of humanity. Even in hardship, this perspective reminds us that we are part of something greater than ourselves. By contributing to the well-being of others, we find meaning that transcends individual pain.

This universality is also reflected in religious and spiritual teachings. Many faiths view suffering as a pathway to growth, whether through redemption, enlightenment, or the fulfillment of divine purpose. These traditions offer not only comfort but also a framework for understanding the role of hardship in the human experience.

Meaning as a Source of Resilience

Ultimately, meaning is not just a way to endure hardship—it is a way to transcend it. When we find purpose in our pain, we transform it from a source of despair into a source of strength. This transformation is at the heart of resilience. It allows us to move forward not despite adversity but because of it, carrying with us the lessons and insights that hardship has revealed.

As we navigate the challenges of life, the search for meaning reminds us that even in our darkest moments, there is light to be found. It invites us to embrace adversity not as an end but as a beginning—a chance to discover who we are, what we value, and how we can make a difference. Through meaning, we find not only the courage to persevere but also the wisdom to thrive.

Overcoming Fear and Doubt

Fear and doubt, like shadows cast by adversity, can obscure our path forward. They whisper of danger and inadequacy, urging us to retreat into safety and certainty. Yet, these emotions are not enemies to be vanquished but signals to be understood. To overcome fear and doubt is to learn their language, harness their energy, and transform them into catalysts for courage and clarity.

The Roots of Fear and Doubt

Fear is one of humanity's most primal emotions, a survival mechanism honed over millennia to protect us from threats. In the wild, fear spurred our ancestors to flee predators, seek shelter, and avoid perilous situations. But in the modern world, where threats are often psychological rather than physical, fear can become misaligned with reality. It manifests as anxiety about the unknown, apprehension about failure, or a paralyzing dread of rejection and judgment.

Doubt, often intertwined with fear, arises from our internal narrative—the stories we tell ourselves about our abilities, worth, and potential. While fear warns of external dangers, doubt erodes our confidence from within. It is the voice that questions whether we are good enough, smart enough, or strong enough to face the challenges before us.

Together, fear and doubt can create a powerful barrier to resilience. Yet history and philosophy teach us that these emotions, while potent, are not insurmountable. With self-awareness and deliberate effort, we can confront and transcend them.

Historical Lessons in Courage

History is replete with individuals who faced fear and doubt head-on, transforming these emotions into sources of strength. Consider the story of Harriet Tubman, who escaped slavery only to return repeatedly to guide others to freedom through the Underground Railroad. Each journey was fraught with danger, and the stakes were unimaginably high. Tubman later admitted to feeling fear but emphasized that she refused to let it dictate her actions. "I was the conductor of the Underground Railroad for eight years," she said, "and I can say what most conductors can't say—I never ran my train off the track, and I never lost a passenger."

Tubman's courage did not come from the absence of fear but from her ability to prioritize her mission over her emotions. Her story reminds us that courage is not the elimination of fear but the decision to act despite it.

Another poignant example is Eleanor Roosevelt, who grappled with profound self-doubt throughout her life. As a young woman, she was painfully shy and insecure, yet she went on to become one of the most influential figures of her time. Roosevelt's advice for overcoming fear and doubt is simple yet profound: "You gain strength, courage, and confidence by every experience in which you really stop to look fear in the face. You are able to say to yourself, 'I lived through this horror. I can take the next thing that comes along.'"

Philosophical Insights on Fear and Doubt

Philosophy offers invaluable insights into managing fear and doubt. Stoic philosophers, for instance, recognized that fear often stems from our perception of events rather than the events themselves. Epictetus, a former slave turned philosopher, advised his students to focus on what lies within their control and to let go of concern for external outcomes. "Men are disturbed not by things," he wrote, "but by the views which they take of them."

This Stoic principle encourages us to reframe fear as an opportunity for growth. Instead of fearing failure, we can see it as a chance to learn and improve. Instead of doubting our abilities, we can focus on the effort and discipline required to develop them.

Similarly, Buddhist philosophy emphasizes the impermanence of all things, including fear and doubt. By cultivating mindfulness, we can observe these emotions without becoming consumed by them. This practice helps us recognize that fear and doubt are transient—they arise, linger, and eventually dissipate. Mindfulness creates a mental space where we can respond to these emotions thoughtfully rather than reacting impulsively.

Practical Strategies for Confronting Fear and Doubt

Overcoming fear and doubt begins with self-awareness. By identifying the specific fears and doubts that hold us back, we can begin to address their underlying causes. For example, fear of failure often stems from perfectionism, while doubt about one's abilities may be rooted in a lack of experience or self-compassion.

Visualization is a powerful technique for confronting fear. Athletes and performers often use visualization to mentally rehearse their actions, imagining themselves succeeding despite challenges. This practice not only builds confidence but also desensitizes the brain to fear triggers, making them feel less overwhelming in real-life situations.

Another effective strategy is gradual exposure. If fear arises from the unknown, breaking a daunting challenge into smaller, manageable steps can make it feel less intimidating. For instance, if public speaking provokes anxiety, starting with a small audience of trusted friends can build confidence over time.

Self-compassion is equally important in overcoming doubt. Dr. Kristin Neff, a leading researcher on self-compassion, emphasizes the importance of treating ourselves with kindness during moments of struggle. By acknowledging our humanity and reframing mistakes as opportunities for growth, we weaken the hold of self-doubt and foster resilience.

Harnessing Fear as a Source of Strength

While fear and doubt can feel like barriers, they also hold the potential to fuel growth and motivation. Fear, in particular, signals what matters most to us—our aspirations, values, and dreams. By leaning into this signal, we can use fear as a guide to what we truly care about and what challenges are worth pursuing.

For example, an entrepreneur launching a new venture may fear failure, but this fear also reflects their passion and ambition. By acknowledging the fear and channeling it into preparation and perseverance, they can turn a potential obstacle into a source of energy.

Similarly, doubt can inspire humility and a commitment to self-improvement. Recognizing our limitations is not a sign of weakness but an invitation to learn and grow. When approached with curiosity and determination, doubt becomes a catalyst for personal development.

Fearless, Not Fear-Free

The journey to overcoming fear and doubt is not about eradicating these emotions—they are an inherent part of the human experience. Instead, it is about cultivating the resilience to move forward despite them. It is about recognizing that fear and doubt, while uncomfortable, are also opportunities to deepen our understanding of ourselves and our potential.

As we navigate life's challenges, we can take inspiration from those who have faced fear and doubt with courage and grace. Their stories remind us that we, too, have the capacity to rise above our insecurities and limitations. By embracing fear and doubt as teachers rather than adversaries, we unlock a wellspring of strength and wisdom, enabling us to face the future with confidence and resolve.

Rebuilding After Setbacks

Failure is a universal experience, yet its sting can leave us questioning our worth, purpose, and direction. While setbacks often feel like endings, they are, in reality, opportunities for renewal and transformation. Rebuilding after a failure is not about erasing the past but about using it as a foundation for something stronger. The process requires courage, reflection, and an unwavering belief in the possibility of growth.

The Resilience of Renewal

History is filled with stories of individuals who have not only recovered from setbacks but used them as stepping stones to remarkable achievements. One striking example is the story of Thomas Edison, whose path to inventing the light bulb was marked by thousands of failed experiments. When asked about these failures, Edison famously remarked, "I have not failed. I've just found 10,000 ways that won't work." His perspective underscores a critical truth: failure is not a verdict but a step in the process of creation.

Edison's story illustrates the power of persistence and the ability to reframe setbacks as valuable lessons. Rather than succumbing to despair, he approached each failure with curiosity and determination, ultimately achieving success that transformed the modern world.

Another example is J.K. Rowling, who faced numerous rejections before publishing the first Harry Potter book. At her lowest point, she was a single mother living on welfare, yet she continued to write, fueled by her passion and belief in her story. Today, her books have touched millions, and her journey serves as a testament to the transformative power of perseverance.

These stories remind us that setbacks, no matter how discouraging, are not the end of the road. They are moments of recalibration, challenging us to adapt, innovate, and rebuild with new-found strength.

The Philosophy of Starting Anew

Philosophy offers profound insights into the process of rebuilding. The Stoics, who emphasized the importance of resilience, believed that failure was an inevitable part of life and an opportunity for growth. Seneca, a Roman statesman and philosopher, wrote, "Every new beginning comes from some other beginning's end." This perspective encourages us to view setbacks not as failures but as transitions—necessary phases in the journey toward self-improvement.

In Eastern philosophy, the concept of *kaizen*, or continuous improvement, offers a practical framework for rebuilding. Rooted in Japanese culture, *kaizen* emphasizes incremental progress over time. Rather than striving for perfection, it advocates for small, consistent steps toward a goal. This approach fosters patience and persistence, allowing individuals to rebuild with intention and purpose.

These philosophical traditions remind us that rebuilding is not about erasing the past but about integrating its lessons into a stronger, wiser foundation.

Practical Steps for Rebuilding Confidence

Rebuilding after a setback begins with restoring confidence. When failure undermines our belief in ourselves, the path forward can feel uncertain. However, confidence is not a fixed trait—it is a skill that can be cultivated through deliberate action.

The first step is reflection. Taking time to analyze what went wrong allows us to identify patterns, avoid repeating mistakes, and extract valuable lessons. This process requires honesty and self-compassion. Rather than dwelling on what could have been, we focus on what can be learned and applied moving forward.

Once we understand the factors that contributed to the setback, the next step is setting achievable goals. Rebuilding is a process, and success comes from small, manageable victories that restore momentum and confidence. For example, an athlete recovering from an injury might begin with basic exercises before gradually increasing intensity. Each step forward reinforces their belief in their abilities and their potential for recovery.

Support is another crucial component of rebuilding. Sharing our struggles with trusted friends, mentors, or coaches can provide encouragement, perspective, and guidance. Others often see our potential more clearly than we do in moments of doubt, and their belief in us can reignite our own confidence.

Embracing Opportunity in Setbacks

Setbacks often reveal opportunities that were previously hidden. While the initial pain of failure can be blinding, it can also force us to reassess our priorities, uncover new strengths, and explore different paths. Many individuals who have faced professional or personal setbacks describe these moments as turning points—times when they discovered new passions, reevaluated their goals, or developed skills they never realized they needed.

Consider the story of Oprah Winfrey, who was fired from her first television job and told she was "unfit for TV." This rejection could have ended her career, but instead, it propelled her toward creating a platform that would redefine daytime television and inspire millions. Winfrey's ability to turn a setback into an opportunity illustrates the transformative power of resilience and reinvention.

In our own lives, setbacks can prompt us to ask important questions: What truly matters to me? What strengths have I overlooked? What new opportunities can I pursue? By shifting our focus from what we have lost to what we can gain, we open the door to new possibilities.

The Role of Time and Patience

Rebuilding is not an overnight process. It requires patience and a willingness to embrace the discomfort of starting over. In moments of frustration, it can be helpful to remember that growth takes time and that setbacks, while painful, are temporary.

Nature offers a powerful metaphor for this process. After a wildfire, the forest floor may appear barren, but beneath the surface, seeds are germinating, and new life is beginning to emerge. Over time, the forest regrows, often more vibrant and diverse than before. Similarly, rebuilding after a setback involves cultivating the conditions for growth, even when progress feels slow or invisible.

Patience also means forgiving ourselves for mistakes and setbacks along the way. The journey is rarely linear, and resilience requires us to navigate its twists and turns with grace and determination.

Rebuilding as a Creative Act

Ultimately, rebuilding is a creative act. It is an opportunity to reimagine our lives, redefine our goals, and rediscover our strengths. Each step forward is an act of creation, a testament to our ability to shape our future regardless of the past.

This process is beautifully encapsulated in the Japanese art of *kintsugi*, or "golden joinery." In *kintsugi*, broken pottery is repaired with gold, creating pieces that are more beautiful and valuable for having been broken. The cracks, rather than being hidden, are celebrated as part of the object's history. *Kintsugi* teaches us that our setbacks and scars are not flaws to be concealed but sources of strength and beauty to be embraced.

As we rebuild after setbacks, we have the opportunity to apply this principle to our own lives. By honoring our struggles and integrating their lessons, we create a future that is richer, stronger, and more meaningful than what came before.

A Foundation for Growth

Rebuilding after a setback is one of the most challenging yet rewarding journeys we can undertake. It requires courage to confront failure, resilience to rise again, and vision to imagine a brighter future. But as history, philosophy, and personal experience teach us, setbacks are not the end of the story. They are the moments that define it.

Through reflection, action, and patience, we can transform failure into a foundation for growth, building a life that is not only resilient but truly extraordinary. The process may be difficult, but the rewards—renewed confidence, deeper wisdom, and a stronger sense of purpose—are immeasurable.

CHAPTER 3: ANCHORS OF INNER STRENGTH – VALUES THAT SUSTAIN US

Defining Your Core Values

In the chaotic swirl of modern life, where external pressures often dictate priorities and actions, core values serve as an anchor. They are the deeply held principles that guide our decisions, shape our character, and define who we are. Yet, many people navigate life without ever consciously identifying their values, leaving them adrift in moments of uncertainty. Understanding and embracing your core values is not merely an exercise in introspection—it is a foundational step toward inner strength and resilience.

The Role of Values in Shaping Our Lives

Values influence every aspect of our lives, often operating below the surface of conscious awareness. They inform how we interact with others, how we respond to challenges, and how we measure success. When we align our actions with our values, we experience a sense of integrity and purpose. Conversely, when we stray from them, we may feel disoriented, conflicted, or unfulfilled.

Consider the story of Mahatma Gandhi, whose unwavering commitment to the values of non-violence and truth transformed a nation and inspired the world. Gandhi's adherence to these principles was not merely a political strategy; it was a reflection of his deepest beliefs about justice and humanity. Even in the face of imprisonment and violence, Gandhi remained steadfast, drawing strength from his values. His life demonstrates that core values are not just moral ideals but powerful sources of resilience and clarity.

While most of us may not face the same monumental challenges as Gandhi, the principle remains the same: when we define and live by our values, we create a compass that steadies us through life's uncertainties.

The Process of Defining Your Values

Identifying your core values is a deeply personal journey, one that requires introspection and honesty. It begins with asking fundamental questions about what matters most to you:

- What principles guide your decisions when no

one is watching?

- What traits do you admire in others and aspire to embody?

- What brings you a sense of fulfillment and purpose?

- What, if lost, would leave you feeling disconnected from yourself?

These questions invite you to look beyond societal expectations or external achievements and focus on the qualities and beliefs that resonate with your authentic self.

For some, values may be shaped by formative experiences. A person who grew up witnessing acts of generosity may hold kindness as a core value. Another who overcame significant adversity may value resilience or perseverance. Reflecting on pivotal moments in your life — both triumphant and challenging — can reveal patterns and priorities that point to your underlying values.

The Power of Clarity

Once identified, core values act as a lens through which you can evaluate decisions and actions. This clarity simplifies life's complexities, enabling you to navigate challenges with confidence and consistency. When faced with a difficult choice, asking, "Does this align with my values?" can provide a clear path forward.

Consider the example of Rosa Parks, whose decision to remain seated on a segregated bus in Montgomery, Alabama, was a profound act of alignment with her values. Parks valued equality and dignity, and her refusal to yield her seat was not a spontaneous act but a deliberate choice grounded in her principles. Her clarity of purpose not only empowered her in that moment but also sparked a movement that changed the course of history.

For those of us navigating more ordinary circumstances, the principle is the same. Whether deciding on a career path, resolving a conflict, or managing relationships, grounding your choices in your core values ensures that your actions reflect your true self.

The Intersection of Values and Resilience

Core values do more than guide decisions—they also provide a foundation for resilience. In moments of hardship, values remind us of what truly matters, offering a sense of stability and purpose. Viktor Frankl, whose experiences in Nazi concentration camps led to profound insights on human resilience, observed that individuals who survived such unimaginable suffering often did so by clinging to their values. For Frankl, the value of love and the belief in the meaningfulness of life sustained him, even in the face of despair.

This connection between values and resilience is also evident in the lives of everyday people. A parent enduring long hours at work to provide for their family may find strength in the value of responsibility. A student striving to overcome academic challenges may draw inspiration from a commitment to personal growth. In both cases, values serve as a wellspring of motivation and endurance.

Practical Steps to Living Your Values

Defining your values is only the beginning; the true challenge lies in living them consistently. This requires intentionality and reflection. Start by identifying specific actions that align with your values. For example, if integrity is a core value, this might mean being honest in difficult conversations or upholding commitments even when inconvenient.

Journaling can be a powerful tool for tracking your alignment with your values. Reflecting on daily actions and decisions helps you recognize patterns, celebrate successes, and address areas where you may have fallen short. Over time, this practice reinforces the habit of living in accordance with your values.

It is also important to communicate your values to others. By articulating what matters most to you, you create opportunities for deeper con-nections and mutual understanding. Whether in personal relationships or professional settings, sharing your values fosters trust and collabo-ration.

The Courage to Reassess

Values are not static; they evolve as we grow and encounter new experiences. Periodically reassessing your values ensures that they continue to reflect your authentic self. This process requires courage, as it may involve letting go of beliefs that no longer serve you or embracing new principles that challenge your comfort zone.

For example, a person who once prioritized career success above all else may, after becoming a parent, shift their focus to family and balance. Recognizing and honoring this evolution is not a betrayal of past values but a reflection of growth and self-awareness.

Building a Life Anchored in Values

When we define and live by our core values, we create a life that is both purposeful and resilient. Values act as a steady anchor, grounding us in times of change and guiding us through uncertainty. They remind us of who we are and what we stand for, offering clarity and strength in even the most challenging circumstances.

As you embark on the journey of defining your

values, remember that this process is not about perfection but about alignment. It is about bridging the gap between who you are and who you aspire to be, creating a life that reflects your deepest truths. In doing so, you not only cultivate inner strength but also inspire those around you to do the same.

The Role of Integrity in Resilience

Integrity is often described as the alignment between one's actions and values. It is the commitment to living authentically, even when doing so is inconvenient or difficult. Yet, integrity is more than a moral ideal—it is a cornerstone of resilience. When we remain true to our principles, we build inner strength, foster trust in ourselves and others, and cultivate the resolve to navigate life's challenges with dignity and purpose.

Integrity as a Source of Inner Strength

At its core, integrity is about consistency. It requires that we act in accordance with our beliefs, regardless of external pressures or personal gain. This consistency creates a sense of coherence in our lives, grounding us in times of uncertainty. When we act with integrity, we affirm our values and strengthen our identity, which becomes a source of resilience in the face of adversity.

Consider the example of Nelson Mandela, who spent 27 years in prison for opposing apartheid in South Africa. During this time, Mandela was offered early release on multiple occasions if he agreed to renounce his political stance. Despite the immense personal cost, Mandela refused, choosing instead to remain true to his principles. His unwavering integrity not only sustained him through years of hardship but also became a beacon of hope and strength for millions. Mandela's story illustrates how living in alignment with one's values can provide the clarity and resolve needed to endure even the most daunting challenges.

Integrity is not limited to monumental acts of courage; it is equally essential in everyday decisions. Whether standing up for a colleague at work, admitting a mistake, or honoring a commitment, acts of integrity reinforce our inner resolve. They remind us that we are capable of acting with courage and authenticity, which strengthens our confidence and resilience over time.

The Consequences of Compromising Integrity

While integrity builds strength, compromising it often leads to internal conflict and diminished resilience. When we act in ways that contradict our values, we create a gap between who we are and who we aspire to be. This gap, known in psychology as cognitive dissonance, can result in feelings of guilt, shame, or self-doubt.

For example, someone who values honesty but tells a significant lie may experience ongoing stress as they try to reconcile their actions with their principles. This dissonance not only drains emotional energy but also undermines the trust they place in themselves. Over time, repeated compromises of integrity can erode self-esteem and make it harder to confront challenges with confidence.

On a broader scale, the erosion of integrity can have societal consequences. Historical examples, such as corporate scandals or political corruption, demonstrate how compromises in integrity can lead to widespread mistrust and systemic collapse. These examples underscore the importance of integrity not only for individual resilience but also for collective well-being.

Philosophical Reflections on Integrity

Philosophers across cultures have long emphasized the role of integrity in leading a resilient and meaningful life. Aristotle, the ancient Greek philosopher, argued that integrity is a key component of *eudaimonia*—a state of flourishing or living well. For Aristotle, living virtuously and in accordance with one's principles was essential for achieving true happiness and resilience.

Similarly, Confucian philosophy places great importance on the concept of *yi*, often translated as righteousness or moral rectitude. Confucius taught that integrity in thought and action creates harmony within oneself and in relationships with others. By adhering to principles of honesty, fairness, and responsibility, individuals contribute to the stability and resilience of their communities.

These philosophical traditions remind us that

integrity is not merely about avoiding wrong-
doing; it is about actively embodying our values
and fulfilling our potential. It is through this
commitment to authenticity that we build a life
of strength and purpose.

Cultivating Integrity in Daily Life

Living with integrity is a daily practice, one
that requires self-awareness, courage, and accountability. The first step is to clearly define
your values, as explored in the previous section.
Knowing what matters most to you provides a
foundation for making decisions that align with
your principles.

Once your values are clear, the next step is to
act on them consistently. This may involve making difficult choices, such as standing up for
what you believe in or acknowledging mistakes.
For example, a leader who values transparency
might choose to share challenging news with
their team rather than withholding information
to protect their image. While such actions may
be uncomfortable in the moment, they ultimately build trust and strengthen both individual
and collective resilience.

Accountability is also crucial in maintaining integrity. This involves reflecting on your actions and being willing to correct course when necessary. Journaling or seeking feedback from trusted friends or mentors can help you stay aligned with your values. When lapses in integrity occur, addressing them openly and learning from the experience reinforces your commitment to authenticity.

The Interplay Between Integrity and Trust

Integrity not only strengthens our relationship with ourselves but also fosters trust in our relationships with others. When we act with integrity, we demonstrate reliability, honesty, and respect—qualities that are essential for building strong connections. These connections, in turn, provide emotional support and a sense of belonging, both of which are critical for resilience.

Trust, however, is fragile. Compromising integrity can damage relationships and create barriers to collaboration and mutual understanding. Rebuilding trust after a breach requires consistent effort, transparency, and a willingness to take responsibility for one's actions. While challenging, this process can lead to deeper relationships and a renewed commitment to integrity.

The Courage to Uphold Integrity

Upholding integrity often requires courage, especially in situations where doing so comes with personal or professional risks. Speaking out against injustice, resisting peer pressure, or admitting to a mistake can feel daunting, but these actions reaffirm our commitment to our values and strengthen our resilience.

The courage to act with integrity is beautifully captured in the story of Malala Yousafzai, who, as a teenager, advocated for girls' education in the face of violent opposition from the Taliban. Despite being targeted and critically injured, Malala remained steadfast in her principles, becoming a global symbol of courage and resilience. Her story reminds us that integrity is not about perfection but about the willingness to stand firm in our beliefs, even when the stakes are high.

Integrity as a Lifelong Practice

Integrity is not a destination but a journey—a lifelong practice of aligning actions with values, learning from missteps, and striving for authenticity. It is through this practice that we build a foundation of inner strength, one that sustains us in moments of adversity and inspires us in times of opportunity.

As we navigate the complexities of life, integrity serves as both a guide and a refuge. It reminds us of who we are, what we stand for, and what we are capable of achieving. By committing to this principle, we not only strengthen our own resilience but also contribute to a world built on trust, respect, and authenticity.

Purpose as a Pillar of Strength

In life's most challenging moments, the presence or absence of a clear sense of purpose can mean the difference between despair and resilience. Purpose acts as an anchor, grounding us amidst uncertainty and providing the motivation to press forward when the path ahead feels insurmountable. It is not merely a lofty ideal but a

practical source of strength—one that gives our
efforts meaning and our struggles significance.
By understanding and cultivating purpose, we
unlock a powerful tool for enduring difficulties
and achieving fulfillment.

The Transformative Power of Purpose

Purpose gives shape to our actions, aligning
them with something greater than immediate
gratification or fleeting success. It provides a
sense of direction, turning hardship into an opportunity for growth and setbacks into stepping
stones. History is rich with examples of individuals whose unwavering sense of purpose enabled them to endure unimaginable difficulties
and emerge stronger.

One of the most striking examples is Viktor
Frankl, the Holocaust survivor and psychiatrist whose philosophy centers on the power of
meaning. In his seminal work, *Man's Search for
Meaning*, Frankl reflects on his time in Nazi concentration camps, where he observed that those
who survived often had a deep sense of purpose.
For some, it was the hope of reuniting with
loved ones; for others, it was the determination

to complete unfinished work or contribute to society in the future. Frankl himself was sustained by the desire to finish his manuscript and share his ideas about meaning with the world. "Life is never made unbearable by circumstances," he wrote, "but only by lack of meaning and purpose."

Frankl's insights underscore the resilience that comes from having a clear "why." Purpose transforms suffering into a challenge to be met, rather than a burden to be endured. It shifts the focus from what is happening to us to what we can contribute or achieve despite it.

Philosophical Perspectives on Purpose

Philosophers across cultures have long recognized the role of purpose in human resilience and fulfillment. Aristotle, for instance, viewed purpose as central to living a virtuous and flourishing life. His concept of *telos*, or an ultimate goal, emphasizes that everything in nature has a purpose, and that living in alignment with one's *telos* leads to true happiness. For Aristotle, purpose was not just about personal ambition but about contributing to the greater good.

In Eastern philosophy, the idea of purpose is deeply intertwined with service and connection. The Hindu concept of *dharma* refers to one's duty or role in life, which is shaped by personal strengths, circumstances, and societal needs. Living in accordance with one's *dharma* is seen as essential for both personal fulfillment and the harmony of the broader community. Similarly, in Buddhism, the Eightfold Path encourages individuals to pursue "right livelihood" and "right intention," aligning their actions with a sense of higher purpose.

These philosophical traditions remind us that purpose is not simply about individual success but about aligning our actions with values, principles, and the greater good. It is this alignment that gives purpose its power to sustain us through difficulties.

Purpose as a Source of Resilience

When we face hardship, a strong sense of purpose can act as a wellspring of resilience. It provides a reason to endure, even when the circumstances seem overwhelming. Purpose offers clarity, reminding us of what truly matters and helping us prioritize our efforts. It also fosters hope, as it connects us to a vision of the future that is worth striving for.

Consider the story of Malala Yousafzai, who became a global advocate for girls' education after surviving an assassination attempt by the Taliban. Despite the physical and emotional trauma she endured, Malala's sense of purpose only grew stronger. Her commitment to ensuring that all children have access to education gave her the strength to recover and continue her work. In her words, "When the whole world is silent, even one voice becomes powerful." Malala's story illustrates how purpose not only sustains us through hardship but also amplifies our impact on the world.

Finding Your Purpose

While purpose is undeniably powerful, it is not always easy to identify. Many people struggle with the question, "What is my purpose?" The good news is that purpose does not have to be grand or extraordinary—it simply needs to resonate with your values and aspirations. Purpose can be found in small, meaningful acts as well as in larger, long-term goals.

One way to discover your purpose is to reflect on what brings you joy and fulfillment. What activities make you lose track of time? What causes or issues ignite your passion? Purpose often lies at the intersection of what you love, what you are good at, and what the world needs. For example, someone who loves teaching and has a talent for communication may find purpose in mentoring others, whether professionally or informally.

Another approach is to consider how you can use your experiences to help others. Many individuals who have faced adversity find purpose in supporting others who are going through similar challenges. A cancer survivor might become an advocate for early detection, while someone who has overcome addiction might dedicate themselves to helping others recover.

Finally, purpose can be cultivated through action. Sometimes, we discover our purpose not by thinking about it but by doing. Volunteering, exploring new interests, or pursuing creative projects can reveal passions and strengths that were previously hidden. As the philosopher Søren Kierkegaard observed, "Life can only be understood backwards; but it must be lived forwards." Purpose often becomes clearer as we engage with life and reflect on our experiences.

Living with Purpose

Once you have identified your purpose, the next step is to integrate it into your daily life. This does not necessarily mean making dramatic changes; often, it is about finding ways to align your existing activities with your sense of purpose. For example, someone who values connection might prioritize spending quality time with loved ones, while someone who values creativity might carve out time for artistic expression.

Living with purpose also requires resilience. There will be moments when pursuing your purpose feels challenging or discouraging. In these times, it is important to revisit your "why" and remind yourself of the greater meaning behind your efforts. Surrounding yourself with supportive individuals who share or respect your purpose can provide encouragement and accountability.

Purpose as a Lifelong Journey

Purpose is not static; it evolves as we grow and change. What feels meaningful at one stage of life may shift as our circumstances and priorities change. For this reason, it is important to approach purpose as a lifelong journey rather than a fixed destination. Periodic reflection and recalibration ensure that your purpose remains aligned with your values and aspirations.

At its core, purpose is not about perfection or achievement—it is about connection. It connects us to our values, our communities, and a vision of a better future. It reminds us that even in the face of hardship, our efforts have meaning and our lives have significance. By embracing purpose as a pillar of strength, we not only navigate life's challenges with resilience but also create a legacy of impact and inspiration.

Living in Alignment with Values

Understanding your core values is an essential

first step, but the true power of values lies in living them. When our actions reflect our principles, we create a sense of harmony between who we are and how we engage with the world. This alignment not only fosters resilience but also provides a profound sense of purpose and fulfillment. Living in alignment with values is not always easy, but it is a practice that, when cultivated, forms the foundation of a strong, authentic life.

The Importance of Consistency

Living in alignment with values requires consistency. It is about making choices that reflect your principles, even when those choices are inconvenient or challenging. This consistency strengthens your sense of identity and builds trust—both with yourself and with others. When your words and actions align with your values, you create a solid foundation of integrity, which serves as a wellspring of inner strength.

Take, for example, Mahatma Gandhi, whose life was a testament to living in alignment with his values of nonviolence and truth. Gandhi's consistency in adhering to these principles, even under immense pressure, inspired millions and brought about transformative change. His un-wavering commitment to living his values not only shaped his character but also amplified his impact on the world.

While most of us may not face challenges on the scale of Gandhi's, the principle remains the same: aligning our daily actions with our values fosters a sense of purpose and authenticity that sustains us through difficulties.

The Challenges of Alignment

Living in alignment with values is not without its challenges. There are times when external pressures, conflicting priorities, or fear of judg-ment can make it difficult to stay true to our principles. For instance, someone who values honesty may struggle to be transparent in a situation where doing so could lead to conflict or criticism. Similarly, a person who values kindness might find it difficult to set boundar-ies, fearing that doing so could be perceived as unkind.

These challenges highlight the importance of

self-awareness and intentionality. Recognizing the moments when your actions diverge from your values allows you to course-correct and make adjustments. It also requires acknowledging that perfection is not the goal; what matters is the ongoing effort to align your life with your principles.

Practical Strategies for Alignment

Living in alignment with your values is a practice that unfolds in daily decisions and habits. The following strategies can help you cultivate this alignment, creating a life that reflects your deepest truths:

1. **Reflection and Clarity**: Begin by regularly reflecting on your values and assessing how well your actions align with them. Journaling or meditation can provide a space for this introspection, allowing you to identify areas where you may need to adjust your behaviors or priorities.

2. **Setting Intentions**: Each day, set an intention to live in accordance with a specific value. For example, if compassion is one of your values,

you might decide to perform one act of kindness or approach a difficult conversation with empathy. These small, deliberate actions reinforce your commitment to your principles.

3. Boundaries and Prioritization: Living your values often requires saying no to activities or behaviors that conflict with your principles. Setting boundaries ensures that your time and energy are devoted to what truly matters. For instance, if family is a core value, prioritizing quality time with loved ones over work commitments can help you maintain alignment.

4. Accountability and Feedback: Sharing your values with trusted friends or mentors creates accountability and invites feedback. These relationships can provide support and perspective, helping you stay on track and navigate challenges.

5. Adapting with Flexibility: While consistency is important, it is equally crucial to remain flexible and adaptable. Life is dynamic, and there may be times when your values evolve or when circumstances require you to adjust your approach. Embracing this flexibility allows you to maintain alignment without rigidly clinging to specific actions or outcomes.

The Role of Reflection

Reflection is a cornerstone of living in alignment with values. It provides the opportunity to celebrate successes, learn from missteps, and deepen your understanding of what matters most. Periodic self-assessment ensures that your values remain relevant and that your actions continue to reflect your principles.

Consider the example of Eleanor Roosevelt, who faced numerous personal and professional challenges throughout her life. Roosevelt frequently reflected on her actions and decisions, using her experiences to refine her sense of purpose and values. Her willingness to adapt and grow enabled her to become a powerful advocate for human rights and social justice, living a life deeply aligned with her principles.

For those of us seeking similar alignment, asking questions like "What did I do today that reflects my values?" or "Where can I improve?" can provide valuable insights. This practice fosters self-awareness and encourages intentionality, ensuring that your values remain a guiding force in your life.

The Rewards of Alignment

When you live in alignment with your values, the rewards are profound. Alignment fosters a sense of authenticity and coherence, reducing internal conflict and increasing emotional resilience. It also enhances your relationships, as others are drawn to the consistency and integrity that alignment brings.

Moreover, living your values creates a ripple effect. Your actions inspire others, demonstrating the power of authenticity and encouraging those around you to reflect on their own principles. This influence extends beyond individual relationships, contributing to a culture of trust, respect, and shared purpose.

Alignment as a Lifelong Practice

Living in alignment with values is not a one-time achievement but a lifelong journey. It requires ongoing effort, reflection, and adaptation.

There will be moments of success and moments of challenge, but each step forward deepens your connection to your authentic self.

As you navigate this journey, remember that alignment is not about perfection—it is about progress. Each choice to live your values, no matter how small, strengthens the foundation of your resilience and brings you closer to the life you envision. By committing to this practice, you create a life of purpose, authenticity, and inner strength—one that reflects not only who you are but who you aspire to become.

CHAPTER 4: THE POWER OF PATIENCE – STRENGTH IN STILLNESS

The Art of Waiting

Patience is a virtue that has echoed through time, celebrated by cultures, philosophies, and traditions across the globe. In a world that often demands immediacy, patience stands as a quiet but profound strength—a testament to the power of waiting, enduring, and trusting in the process. Far from being passive, patience is an active virtue, requiring discipline, perspective, and a deep understanding of life's natural rhythms.

Patience in Historical Context

Throughout history, patience has been revered as a hallmark of wisdom and strength. Ancient cultures recognized its value not only in personal growth but also in achieving greater societal harmony. In Ancient Greece, patience was associated with the concept of *sophrosyne*, or self-control, which the philosopher Plato deemed essential for living a virtuous life. Plato believed that mastering impatience allowed individuals to align their actions with reason and moral principles, fostering a sense of balance and inner peace.

In Eastern traditions, patience takes on a spiritual dimension. Buddhism, for instance, identifies patience, or *kshanti*, as one of the six *paramitas* (perfections) necessary for enlightenment. The Buddha taught that patience is not merely enduring hardship but embracing it with understanding and compassion. He compared impatience to a burning coal, noting that the person who holds onto anger or frustration is the one who gets burned. Instead, cultivating patience allows individuals to let go of suffering and approach life's challenges with clarity and composure.

Similarly, the Taoist philosophy of *wu wei*, or effortless action, emphasizes the importance of flowing with life rather than resisting its natural rhythms. Patience, in this context, is about recognizing that some outcomes cannot be forced and that growth often requires time. Laozi, the author of the *Tao Te Ching*, wrote, "Nature does not hurry, yet everything is accomplished." This wisdom encourages us to trust in the unfolding of events, knowing that progress, though gradual, is inevitable.

The Power of Waiting in Action

The art of waiting is vividly illustrated in the story of Abraham Lincoln. Before becoming one of the most revered presidents in American history, Lincoln faced a string of personal and professional failures. From losing his job to enduring multiple electoral defeats, his journey was marked by setbacks. Yet, Lincoln's patience and perseverance allowed him to grow, learn, and ultimately rise to meet the challenges of his time. His story reminds us that patience is not the absence of struggle but the willingness to endure it in pursuit of something greater.

On a larger scale, the construction of the Great Wall of China stands as a testament to collective patience and determination. Spanning centuries, this monumental effort required the work of countless individuals, each contributing to a vision that far exceeded their lifetimes. The Great Wall reminds us that patience is not only about enduring the moment but also about building something enduring—something that transcends the immediate.

Philosophical Reflections on Patience

Philosophers have long pondered the nature of patience and its role in the human experience. The Stoics, for example, viewed patience as an essential element of resilience. Seneca, a Roman philosopher, argued that impatience often stems from unrealistic expectations and a lack of perspective. In his essay *On the Shortness of Life*, Seneca observed that life feels short not because of its brevity but because of how we squander it, rushing from one desire to the next without appreciating the journey. For Seneca, patience was a way to fully engage with life, embracing each moment for its inherent value.

In contrast, Søren Kierkegaard, a 19th-century Danish philosopher, explored the relationship between patience and faith. Kierkegaard believed that patience requires trust in the unknown, a willingness to wait for answers that may not come immediately or even within one's lifetime. This trust, he argued, allows us to endure uncertainty with grace, finding strength in the act of waiting itself.

Patience as a Strength, Not a Weakness

One of the common misconceptions about patience is that it is passive—that it involves simply enduring without action. In reality, patience is an active and deliberate choice. It requires self-discipline, emotional regulation, and the ability to see beyond the immediate. Patience is the parent who listens calmly to their child's frustrations, the artist who spends years perfecting their craft, the leader who resists impulsive decisions in favor of thoughtful strategy.

Consider the metaphor of a seed planted in the ground. The seed does not sprout overnight; it requires time, care, and the right conditions to grow. Yet, beneath the surface, unseen processes are taking place—roots are forming, nutrients are being absorbed, and the potential for growth is being realized. Patience, in this context, is not about inaction but about nurturing and trusting in the unseen work that precedes visible results.

Cultivating Patience in Daily Life

The art of waiting is a skill that can be developed through intentional practice. One way to cultivate patience is through mindfulness—the practice of being present in the moment without judgment. Mindfulness encourages us to observe our thoughts and emotions without reacting to them, creating a space between impulse and action. This practice not only reduces stress but also enhances our ability to approach challenges with composure and perspective.

Another way to develop patience is by embracing delayed gratification. In a world of instant rewards, learning to wait for something meaningful can be transformative. For example, setting long-term goals and working steadily toward them builds both patience and resilience. Whether it's saving for a dream home, mastering a new skill, or fostering a meaningful relationship, the rewards of patience far outweigh the fleeting satisfaction of immediate results.

Finally, cultivating gratitude can help shift our focus from what we lack to what we already have. Gratitude fosters contentment, reducing the restlessness that often fuels impatience. By appreciating the present, we create a foundation of calm and stability that allows us to wait with grace.

The Legacy of Patience

The art of waiting is not simply about enduring time—it is about using time wisely, embracing its lessons, and trusting in its process. Patience teaches us to value the journey as much as the destination, to find strength in stillness, and to appreciate the beauty of life's unfolding.

As we navigate a world that often prioritizes speed and efficiency, the wisdom of patience becomes all the more valuable. It reminds us that some of the most meaningful achievements and experiences cannot be rushed—that their worth lies not only in their outcome but in the time and effort invested in them. By cultivating patience, we not only strengthen our resilience but also enrich our lives, creating a legacy of enduring strength and fulfillment.

Patience as a Strategic Tool

Patience is often perceived as a passive quality—a virtue of those who wait for life to unfold. But history reveals a different truth: patience is a powerful and deliberate strategy. In moments of uncertainty, conflict, or challenge, patience can be the key to transformative success. It is the discipline to wait for the right moment to act, the clarity to see beyond immediate gratification, and the resolve to remain steady in pursuit of a greater goal.

Patience in Wartime Strategy

The annals of history are filled with examples of leaders who wielded patience as a strategic weapon. One of the most celebrated cases is George Washington during the American Revolutionary War. Washington's strategy was not one of immediate confrontation but of calculated endurance. Recognizing that the fledgling American forces could not match the might of the British army in open battle, Washington adopted a strategy of attrition, avoiding decisive engagements and instead focusing on smaller, winnable skirmishes.

This patient approach allowed Washington to preserve his army while wearing down British resources and morale over time. The culmination of this strategy was the decisive victory at Yorktown, which led to American independence. Washington's ability to resist the impulse for immediate glory and instead play the long game demonstrates the power of patience in achieving monumental outcomes.

Similarly, Mahatma Gandhi's campaign for Indian independence exemplifies patience as a tool for societal change. Gandhi's philosophy of *satyagraha*, or nonviolent resistance, relied on the enduring strength of patience. Through peaceful protests, boycotts, and civil disobedience, Gandhi and his followers challenged British rule without resorting to violence, even in the face of brutal suppression. This patient strategy not only won the moral high ground but also garnered global support for India's cause, ultimately leading to independence. Gandhi's approach underscores that patience, when combined with unwavering resolve, can overcome even the most entrenched power structures.

Patience in Scientific Discovery

In the realm of science, patience has been an essential ingredient in groundbreaking discoveries. One of the most iconic examples is Charles Darwin's development of the theory of evolution by natural selection. Darwin's journey toward this revolutionary idea was marked by years of meticulous observation, experimentation, and reflection. After his voyage on the HMS *Beagle*, Darwin spent more than two decades gathering evidence and refining his ideas before publishing *On the Origin of Species* in 1859.

Darwin's patience allowed him to build a robust case for his theory, ensuring that it would withstand scrutiny and revolutionize the scientific understanding of life. His story illustrates that scientific progress often requires the willingness to embrace uncertainty and dedicate years—or even decades—to the pursuit of knowledge.

Another example is Marie Curie, whose discovery of radium and polonium fundamentally changed the field of physics and medicine. Curie's research was a painstaking process, involving years of isolating radioactive elements from tons of pitchblende ore. Her patience and perseverance not only led to groundbreaking discoveries but also earned her two Nobel Prizes. Curie's story reminds us that patience is not the absence of effort but the commitment to sustained, focused work in the face of challenges.

Philosophical Insights on Patience as Strategy

Philosophers have long recognized the strategic value of patience. The Stoics, for instance, emphasized the importance of enduring hardships and waiting for the right moment to act. Epictetus, a Stoic philosopher, advised, "No great thing is created suddenly, any more than a bunch of grapes or a fig. If you tell me that you desire a fig, I answer you that there must be time. Let it first blossom, then bear fruit, then ripen."

This perspective highlights that patience is not passive waiting but an active engagement with the process of growth and development. By understanding the natural rhythms of life, we can align our efforts with the flow of time rather than fighting against it.

In Eastern philosophy, the Taoist principle of *wu wei*—often translated as "non-action" or "effortless action"—underscores the strategic use of patience. Laozi, the author of the *Tao Te Ching*, wrote, "He who stands on tiptoe does not stand firm; he who rushes ahead does not go far." This wisdom suggests that forcing outcomes often leads to instability, while patience allows for steady, sustainable progress.

Modern Applications of Patience as Strategy

The strategic value of patience extends beyond history and philosophy; it is equally relevant in contemporary life. In the business world, leaders who embrace patience often achieve lasting success by focusing on long-term goals rather than short-term gains. Warren Buffett, one of the most successful investors in history, attributes much of his success to patience. Buffett's investment philosophy emphasizes the importance of waiting for the right opportunities and allowing investments to grow over time, rather than succumbing to the pressure of immediate returns.

In personal relationships, patience is a key ingredient for building trust and understanding. Effective communication often requires the patience to listen fully and empathize before responding. This approach fosters deeper connections and resolves conflicts more effectively than reactive behavior.

In creative pursuits, patience allows ideas to mature and evolve. Writers, artists, and innovators often describe moments of inspiration as the result of prolonged periods of reflection and experimentation. By giving their work the time it needs to develop, they create pieces that resonate on a deeper level.

Harnessing Patience in Your Own Life

Cultivating patience as a strategic tool begins with shifting your perspective on time. Instead of viewing time as an obstacle to overcome, see it as an ally in achieving meaningful goals. This shift allows you to approach challenges with a sense of calm and purpose, rather than frustration or haste.

Practicing mindfulness can help you embrace this perspective. By focusing on the present moment, mindfulness reduces the anxiety associated with waiting and enhances your ability to stay engaged with the process. Similarly, setting long-term goals and breaking them into smaller, manageable steps creates a sense of progress, reinforcing your patience along the way.

Finally, remind yourself of the bigger picture. Whether you are navigating a personal challenge, pursuing a professional goal, or striving for societal change, patience allows you to remain steady and committed, even when progress feels slow. Trusting in the process and the passage of time enables you to achieve outcomes that are not only successful but also deeply fulfilling.

The Legacy of Patience

Patience, when wielded strategically, is a force that can shape history, transform lives, and unlock human potential. It requires discipline, foresight, and the courage to endure uncertainty, but its rewards are profound. As the examples of Washington, Gandhi, Darwin, and Curie demonstrate, patience is not a passive quality—it is an active and deliberate choice to persevere, adapt, and trust in the process.

By embracing patience as a strategic tool, we not only navigate challenges with resilience but also create opportunities for growth, discovery, and success that endure far beyond the present moment. In a world that often prioritizes speed and immediacy, the power of patience serves as a timeless reminder that greatness is built not in haste but in steady, purposeful action.

Cultivating Patience in Modern Life

In a world dominated by instant gratification and relentless speed, patience often feels like a forgotten virtue. From same-day deliveries to real-time communication, modern life rewards immediacy, leaving little room for the quiet strength of waiting. Yet, as our lives grow increasingly fast-paced, the ability to cultivate patience becomes not just a necessity but a transformative practice. Patience offers a counterbalance to the stress and urgency of modern life, allowing us to approach challenges with clarity, resilience, and a deeper sense of fulfillment.

The Challenges of Modern Impatience

Our era is defined by convenience and efficiency, but these advancements come at a cost. The constant barrage of notifications, rapid news cycles, and endless streams of information create an environment where attention is fragmented and expectations for immediate results are heightened. Impatience manifests in subtle but pervasive ways—frustration during a slow internet connection, anxiety when waiting for a reply, or dissatisfaction when progress feels slow.

This impatience, however, is not without consequence. Studies have shown that impatience can lead to increased stress, reduced focus, and strained relationships. When we rush through life, we miss the opportunity to fully engage with the present moment, undermining our ability to enjoy the process and learn from it. The antidote lies in cultivating patience—not as a passive endurance but as an active skill that empowers us to navigate life's demands with grace and intention.

Mindfulness: Anchoring in the Present

One of the most effective ways to cultivate patience in modern life is through mindfulness—the practice of being fully present in the moment. Mindfulness encourages us to observe our thoughts, emotions, and surroundings without judgment, creating a space between stimulus and response.

For example, when stuck in traffic or waiting in a long line, instead of succumbing to frustration, mindfulness invites us to shift our focus. We might notice the rhythm of our breath, the colors of the sky, or the sounds around us. This simple act of presence transforms waiting from a source of irritation into an opportunity for reflection and calm.

Scientific research underscores the benefits of mindfulness for cultivating patience. Studies have shown that mindfulness practices reduce stress, improve emotional regulation, and enhance our ability to tolerate uncertainty. By grounding ourselves in the present, we train our minds to let go of the need for immediate results, fostering a sense of acceptance and resilience.

The Practice of Delayed Gratification

Delayed gratification—the ability to resist immediate rewards in favor of greater, long-term benefits—is another cornerstone of patience. This skill is not only essential for achieving meaningful goals but also for cultivating self-control and resilience.

The famous Stanford marshmallow experiment offers a compelling illustration of delayed gratification. In this study, children were given a choice: they could eat one marshmallow immediately or wait 15 minutes to receive two marshmallows. The researchers found that the children who were able to wait tended to have better life outcomes, including higher academic achievement and improved emotional well-being.

In our own lives, practicing delayed gratification can take many forms. It might mean saving money for a future goal rather than indulging in impulse purchases, dedicating time to learning a new skill instead of seeking immediate entertainment, or investing in relationships by prioritizing quality time over superficial interactions. Each act of delayed gratification reinforces our ability to tolerate discomfort and focus on long-term growth, strengthening our capacity for patience.

Reframing Challenges as Opportunities

Patience often requires a shift in perspective— seeing challenges not as obstacles to be overcome but as opportunities for growth. This re-framing allows us to approach setbacks with curiosity rather than frustration, asking, "What can I learn from this?" or "How can this experience make me stronger?"

Consider the example of Thomas Edison, who famously viewed each failed experiment as a step closer to success. When asked about his repeated failures in developing the light bulb, Edison responded, "I have not failed. I've just found 10,000 ways that won't work." His perspective exemplifies the power of patience to transform disappointment into determination.

In our own lives, we can adopt a similar mindset by embracing the process rather than fixating solely on outcomes. Whether we are working toward a career milestone, navigating a difficult relationship, or pursuing personal growth, patience allows us to appreciate the journey and the lessons it brings.

Building Patience Through Daily Habits

Cultivating patience is not an abstract concept; it is a practice that can be integrated into daily life.

Small, intentional actions build the foundation for greater patience over time. For example, setting aside time for reflection—whether through journaling, meditation, or quiet walks—creates space to process emotions and develop perspective.

Engaging in activities that require sustained effort and attention, such as gardening, painting, or cooking, can also strengthen patience. These pursuits remind us that worthwhile outcomes often take time and care, reinforcing the value of persistence and focus.

Another practical habit is practicing gratitude. By focusing on what we have rather than what we lack, gratitude shifts our mindset from impatience to contentment. This shift not only reduces stress but also enhances our ability to approach challenges with a sense of calm and optimism.

Patience in Relationships

Patience is especially vital in our interactions with others. In a world that often prioritizes efficiency over connection, taking the time to listen, understand, and empathize fosters deeper relationships and mutual respect. Patience allows us to navigate conflicts with compassion, recognizing that resolution often requires time and effort.

For example, when faced with a disagreement, instead of reacting impulsively, patience encourages us to pause, reflect, and approach the situation with a willingness to understand the other person's perspective. This approach not only defuses tension but also creates opportunities for growth and reconciliation.

The Transformative Power of Patience

As we cultivate patience in modern life, we begin to experience its transformative effects. Patience reduces stress, enhances focus, and deepens our appreciation for the present moment. It strengthens our relationships, fuels personal growth, and empowers us to pursue long-term goals with resilience and clarity.

In a fast-paced world, patience is a radical act—a declaration that we are not slaves to urgency or instant gratification but masters of our own time and attention. By embracing patience as a practice, we not only navigate life's challenges with greater ease but also unlock its deeper joys and possibilities. In the stillness of patience, we discover the strength to endure, to grow, and to thrive.

The Rewards of Patience

Patience, often seen as a quiet virtue, is one of life's most powerful tools for achieving fulfillment and success. Its rewards are not always immediate or visible, but they are deeply transformative. By embracing patience, we unlock opportunities for personal growth, cultivate meaningful relationships, and achieve lasting success. These rewards remind us that the greatest achievements often require time, perseverance, and a steadfast commitment to the journey.

Patience as the Foundation of Success

Throughout history, patience has been the bedrock of extraordinary accomplishments. Consider the story of Nelson Mandela, who spent 27 years in prison under apartheid before emerging as a global symbol of justice and reconciliation.

Mandela's patience was not passive endurance but an active commitment to his vision of a free and equal South Africa. Despite the immense personal cost, he maintained his resolve, using his time in prison to reflect, learn, and prepare for the challenges ahead. When he finally walked free, Mandela's patience and perseverance had not only sustained him but also inspired a nation to unite and heal.

Mandela's journey illustrates that patience is more than a virtue—it is a strategy for achieving long-term success. By focusing on the bigger picture and resisting the impulse for immediate gratification, we create space for thoughtful decisions, steady progress, and lasting impact. Patience teaches us that success is not about quick wins but about sustained effort and unwavering commitment to our goals.

The Role of Patience in Personal Growth

One of the most profound rewards of patience is its ability to foster personal growth. In a world that often prioritizes speed and efficiency, patience allows us to slow down, reflect, and engage deeply with our experiences. It creates the conditions for self-awareness, resilience, and wisdom—qualities that are essential for navigating life's challenges.

Take the example of artistic pursuits. Whether learning to play a musical instrument, mastering a craft, or writing a novel, patience is an integral part of the creative process. The writer Maya Angelou described this process eloquently, saying, "All great achievements require time." Patience allows artists to embrace imperfections, experiment with new ideas, and persist through setbacks. It transforms frustration into focus and turns challenges into opportunities for growth.

In our own lives, patience can help us develop the resilience needed to overcome obstacles and the humility to accept that progress often comes in small, incremental steps. By cultivating patience, we create the mental and emotional space to learn from our experiences, adapt to changing circumstances, and grow into our fullest potential.

Patience and Deeper Relationships

Relationships thrive on patience. Whether in

friendships, family dynamics, or romantic partnerships, patience fosters understanding, empathy, and trust. It allows us to navigate conflicts with compassion, communicate effectively, and support one another through life's ups and downs.

Consider the story of Fred Rogers, better known as "Mister Rogers," whose gentle patience made him a beloved figure to millions of children and adults. Rogers' ability to listen deeply, respond thoughtfully, and create a safe space for others was rooted in his commitment to patience. His approach reminds us that true connection requires time, presence, and a willingness to meet others where they are.

In our own interactions, practicing patience can transform relationships. It encourages us to listen without interrupting, to empathize without judgment, and to give others the time and space they need to express themselves. These small acts of patience build trust and deepen bonds, creating relationships that are not only resilient but also profoundly fulfilling.

Patience as a Path to Fulfillment

At its core, patience is about finding fulfillment in the journey rather than fixating on the destination. It reminds us that life's most meaningful experiences cannot be rushed — that their value lies not in their speed but in their depth. Patience invites us to savor the present moment, appreciate the beauty of the process, and celebrate small victories along the way.

Philosophers and spiritual traditions have long recognized the connection between patience and fulfillment. The Stoics, for example, viewed patience as a key to tranquility. Seneca wrote, "How much better to endure patiently the ills we cannot avoid than to rage against them and make them worse." This perspective encourages us to accept life's uncertainties with grace, finding peace in the act of waiting rather than in the outcome.

Similarly, Buddhist teachings emphasize the importance of patience in achieving inner peace. The practice of *kshanti*, or forbearance, is one of the six perfections that lead to enlightenment. By cultivating patience, we learn to let go of attachment and aversion, creating a sense of equanimity that allows us to engage with life more fully.

Patience and Long-Term Vision

One of the most significant rewards of patience is its ability to foster a long-term vision. In a culture that often prioritizes immediate results, patience helps us resist the pressure to take shortcuts or settle for superficial achievements. It encourages us to think deeply about what truly matters, set meaningful goals, and work toward them with intention and perseverance.

In the business world, leaders who embrace patience often achieve enduring success. Take the example of Jeff Bezos, the founder of Amazon, who famously prioritized long-term growth over short-term profits. Bezos' patience allowed Amazon to innovate, adapt, and ultimately become one of the most successful companies in history. His story demonstrates that patience is not about complacency but about making deliberate choices that align with a broader vision.

For individuals, cultivating a long-term perspective can transform the way we approach our goals. Whether pursuing a career, building a family, or contributing to a cause, patience allows us to stay focused on our values and aspirations, even in the face of setbacks. It reminds us that true success is not about speed but about sustainability.

The Ripple Effect of Patience

The rewards of patience extend beyond the individual, creating a ripple effect that benefits families, communities, and society as a whole. When we practice patience, we inspire others to do the same, fostering a culture of understanding, cooperation, and shared purpose. Patience encourages us to approach challenges collectively, recognizing that lasting change requires time, effort, and collaboration.

This ripple effect is evident in social movements, where patience often plays a critical role. From the civil rights movement in the United States to the fight for women's suffrage, these efforts required not only courage and determination but also the patience to endure setbacks and persist over years—sometimes decades—to achieve meaningful progress.

Embracing the Rewards of Patience

The rewards of patience are both profound and enduring. They manifest in personal growth, deeper relationships, and the achievement of meaningful goals. They remind us that life's greatest treasures often lie not in the speed of their attainment but in the depth of their experience.

As we embrace patience in our own lives, we cultivate a sense of calm, resilience, and purpose that sustains us through challenges and enriches our journey. In the stillness of patience, we find the strength to persevere, the wisdom to appreciate the present, and the fulfillment that comes from living in alignment with our highest aspirations.

CHAPTER 5: THE RESILIENT MINDSET – HARNESSING THE POWER OF PERSPECTIVE

Seeing Challenges as Opportunities

Life is replete with challenges, some expected and others unforeseen. While adversity can feel like an unwelcome intruder, it also offers an extraordinary opportunity for growth and transformation. The difference lies in perspective: how we choose to see and respond to challenges determines whether they become barriers to our progress or stepping stones to greater resilience. By reframing problems and adopting a growth mindset, we unlock the potential to turn life's trials into opportunities for self-discovery and strength.

The Power of Reframing

Reframing is the art of looking at a situation from a different angle, transforming what seems like an obstacle into a chance for growth. This mental shift allows us to break free from negative thought patterns and approach challenges with curiosity and creativity. Psychologists refer to this as cognitive reappraisal—a strategy that helps individuals regulate their emotions and build resilience.

Take the story of Helen Keller, who lost her sight and hearing as a young child. What could have been an insurmountable barrier became the foundation of her remarkable achievements. With the guidance of her teacher, Anne Sullivan, Keller learned to communicate, eventually becoming a renowned author and activist. Reflecting on her life, Keller wrote, "Although the world is full of suffering, it is also full of the overcoming of it." Her story exemplifies the power of reframing—turning adversity into a source of purpose and strength.

The Growth Mindset: A Catalyst for Resilience

Central to reframing challenges is the concept of a growth mindset, a term popularized by psychologist Carol Dweck. A growth mindset is the belief that abilities and intelligence can be developed through effort, learning, and perseverance. This perspective contrasts with a fixed mindset, which assumes that traits are innate and unchangeable.

Dweck's research demonstrates that individuals with a growth mindset are more likely to embrace challenges, persist through difficulties, and learn from failure. They view setbacks not as indicators of inadequacy but as opportunities to improve. This mindset is a cornerstone of resilience, empowering us to face adversity with determination and adaptability.

Historical figures like Thomas Edison embodied the growth mindset. Edison famously remarked, "I have not failed. I've just found 10,000 ways that won't work." His relentless experimentation and refusal to see failure as a permanent state led to the invention of the light bulb, revolutionizing the modern world. Edison's approach reminds us that challenges are not endpoints but stepping stones on the path to success.

Philosophical Foundations of Resilience

The idea of seeing challenges as opportunities is deeply rooted in philosophical traditions. The Stoics, for instance, embraced the concept of *amor fati*, or "love of fate," which encourages individuals to accept and even embrace the challenges that life presents. Marcus Aurelius, the Roman emperor and philosopher, wrote in his *Meditations*, "What stands in the way becomes the way." This perspective urges us to view obstacles not as hindrances but as integral parts of our journey.

Similarly, Buddhist philosophy teaches that suffering is an inherent part of life but that it also provides an opportunity for growth and enlightenment. The practice of mindfulness helps individuals observe their thoughts and emotions without judgment, allowing them to reframe challenges as lessons rather than burdens. By cultivating acceptance and awareness, we learn to navigate adversity with grace and resilience.

Practical Steps for Reframing Challenges

While the concept of reframing is powerful, putting it into practice requires intentional effort. The first step is to recognize and acknowledge the challenge. Denying or avoiding difficulties only prolongs their impact. Instead, we can ask ourselves, "What can I learn from this experience?" or "How can this challenge help me grow?"

Consider the example of a professional setback,

such as being passed over for a promotion. While the initial reaction may be disappointment or frustration, reframing allows us to see the situation as an opportunity to identify areas for growth. Perhaps it reveals a need to develop new skills, build stronger relationships, or clarify long-term goals. By focusing on what we can control and learn, we transform the setback into a springboard for progress.

Another practical technique is to seek alternative perspectives. Talking with trusted friends, mentors, or colleagues can provide valuable insights and help us see challenges in a new light. For example, a personal conflict might feel insurmountable until someone helps us understand the other person's point of view, opening the door to resolution and mutual understanding.

The Role of Resilience in Reframing

Reframing challenges requires resilience—the ability to adapt and thrive in the face of adversity. Resilience is not about avoiding hardship but about developing the mental and emotional tools to navigate it effectively. This includes cultivating self-awareness, building strong relationships, and maintaining a sense of purpose.

One way to strengthen resilience is through gratitude. By focusing on what we have rather than what we lack, gratitude shifts our perspective and helps us see challenges as part of a broader context. For instance, while a difficult project at work might be stressful, gratitude for supportive colleagues or opportunities for growth can reframe the experience as a positive challenge.

Resilience also involves embracing the process rather than fixating on the outcome. When we view challenges as opportunities for learning and development, we become less attached to immediate results and more invested in the journey. This mindset not only reduces stress but also enhances our ability to find meaning in adversity.

The Long-Term Rewards of Reframing

Seeing challenges as opportunities has profound long-term benefits. It fosters a sense of agency, reminding us that we have the power to shape our experiences and grow from them. This sense of control enhances our confidence and reduces feelings of helplessness or victimhood.

Moreover, reframing challenges helps us build a narrative of resilience. Each time we overcome a difficulty, we add to a mental archive of success stories, reinforcing our belief in our ability to handle future obstacles. This positive feedback loop creates a foundation of inner strength that supports us throughout life.

Inspiring a Culture of Resilience

The practice of reframing challenges is not only an individual endeavor—it can also inspire and strengthen communities. When leaders model resilience and encourage others to see challenges as opportunities, they create an environment of optimism and growth. This culture of resilience fosters collaboration, innovation, and shared purpose.

For example, during the Great Depression, President Franklin D. Roosevelt's message of hope and resilience galvanized a nation. His emphasis on collective effort and perseverance helped millions of Americans reframe their struggles as opportunities to rebuild and thrive. Roosevelt's leadership demonstrates the transformative power of perspective at both individual and societal levels.

Embracing Challenges with Courage and Curiosity

Reframing challenges is not about denying their difficulty but about approaching them with courage and curiosity. It is about asking, "What is this experience teaching me?" and "How can I use this to grow stronger?" By shifting our focus from what is lost to what can be gained, we unlock the potential for resilience and transformation.

As we navigate the inevitable ups and downs of life, the ability to see challenges as opportunities becomes an essential skill. It empowers us to face adversity with confidence, turn setbacks into stepping stones, and create a life rich with growth, meaning, and fulfillment. Through reframing, we discover that challenges are not obstacles to be feared but opportunities to be embraced—a testament to the strength and resilience of the human spirit.

The Role of Optimism in Resilience

Optimism is often misunderstood as a naive or unrealistic outlook on life, but true optimism is far more nuanced and powerful. It is not about ignoring difficulties or pretending everything is perfect; rather, it is the belief that challenges can be overcome and that better days lie ahead. This mindset plays a crucial role in resilience, providing the emotional fuel and mental clarity needed to persevere through adversity. Supported by psychological studies and exemplified throughout history, optimism emerges as a cornerstone of the resilient mindset.

The Science of Optimism

Research in psychology underscores the profound impact of optimism on resilience and well-being. One of the most influential studies on optimism comes from Dr. Martin Seligman, a pioneer of positive psychology. Seligman's work demonstrates that optimistic individuals tend to interpret setbacks as temporary, specific, and external, while pessimistic individuals view them as permanent, pervasive, and personal.

This difference in perspective significantly influences how people respond to adversity.

For example, consider someone who loses their job. An optimist might view the situation as a temporary setback caused by external factors, using it as an opportunity to reassess their career goals and seek new opportunities. A pessimist, on the other hand, might see it as a reflection of their unworthiness, leading to feelings of hopelessness and inaction. Over time, these patterns of thinking shape not only emotional resilience but also tangible outcomes, as optimistic individuals are more likely to take proactive steps toward improvement.

Studies also show that optimism is linked to better physical health, higher levels of motivation, and increased longevity. These benefits stem from the ability of optimism to reduce stress and encourage adaptive coping strategies, such as problem-solving and seeking social support. In short, optimism is not just a mental exercise—it has profound effects on every aspect of life.

Historical Examples of Optimism in Action

History offers countless examples of individuals who harnessed the power of optimism to persevere and inspire others. One of the most striking is the story of Winston Churchill during World War II. Faced with seemingly insurmountable odds, Churchill's unwavering optimism became a beacon of hope for the British people. His famous speeches, filled with defiant confidence and a refusal to surrender, rallied a nation during its darkest hours. Churchill's optimism was not blind faith—it was a deliberate choice to focus on the possibility of victory and to inspire others to believe in that vision.

Another powerful example is Malala Yousafzai, the Pakistani activist who survived an assassination attempt by the Taliban for advocating girls' education. Despite the trauma and danger she faced, Malala's optimism never wavered. She continued her advocacy on a global scale, driven by the belief that change was possible. "Let us remember," she said, "one book, one pen, one child, and one teacher can change the world." Her story illustrates how optimism, grounded in hope and action, can fuel resilience and create lasting impact.

Philosophical Foundations of Optimism

Philosophy, too, offers insights into the transformative power of optimism. The Stoics, for instance, emphasized the importance of focusing on what we can control and maintaining a positive outlook in the face of challenges. Marcus Aurelius, the Roman emperor and Stoic philosopher, wrote, "You have power over your mind—not outside events. Realize this, and you will find strength." This perspective encourages us to view difficulties as opportunities for growth and to trust in our ability to navigate them.

Similarly, Buddhist teachings emphasize the role of hope and intention in cultivating resilience. The concept of *bodhicitta*, or the aspiration to achieve enlightenment for the benefit of all beings, reflects an optimistic vision of personal and collective transformation. By focusing on the potential for positive change, individuals can transcend immediate difficulties and find meaning in their struggles.

Practical Applications of Optimism

Optimism is not an innate trait—it is a skill that can be cultivated through deliberate practice. One of the most effective ways to develop optimism is by challenging negative thought patterns. When faced with a setback, ask yourself: Is this truly permanent? Are there factors beyond my control influencing this situation? What steps can I take to improve it? By reframing negative assumptions, you can shift your perspective and find hope in even the most challenging circumstances.

Another powerful tool is gratitude. Practicing gratitude shifts your focus from what is lacking to what is present, creating a foundation for optimism. For example, keeping a daily gratitude journal can help you identify and appreciate the positive aspects of your life, no matter how small. Over time, this practice rewires your brain to notice opportunities and solutions rather than obstacles.

Visualization is another technique for fostering optimism. By imagining a positive outcome and the steps required to achieve it, you reinforce your belief in your ability to overcome challenges. For instance, an athlete preparing for a competition might visualize themselves performing at their best, building both confidence and motivation.

The Balance Between Optimism and Realism

While optimism is essential for resilience, it must be balanced with realism. Unrealistic optimism—ignoring potential risks or dismissing valid concerns—can lead to poor decision-making and unnecessary setbacks. True optimism involves acknowledging challenges while maintaining faith in your ability to address them.

This balanced approach is evident in the story of Ernest Shackleton, the Antarctic explorer whose ship, the *Endurance*, became trapped in ice. Shackleton's optimism and determination were critical in keeping his crew motivated and united during their ordeal. At the same time, his pragmatic decisions—such as rationing supplies and planning meticulous escape routes—ensured their survival. Shackleton's leadership demonstrates that optimism, when paired with realism, becomes a powerful force for overcoming adversity.

The Ripple Effect of Optimism

Optimism is not only a personal asset—it also has a ripple effect on those around us. When we approach challenges with hope and confidence, we inspire others to do the same. This collective resilience fosters a sense of community and shared purpose, amplifying the impact of optimism.

Consider the example of leaders during times of crisis. Whether rallying a team, supporting a family, or guiding a nation, leaders who exude optimism create a sense of possibility and encourage others to persevere. This ripple effect extends beyond individual relationships, shaping cultures and communities that thrive in the face of adversity.

Embracing Optimism as a Resilient Mindset

Optimism is not about denying difficulties or pretending that everything will always go as planned. It is about choosing to believe in the possibility of growth, learning, and positive outcomes. By cultivating optimism, we strengthen our ability to face challenges with courage and determination, transforming setbacks into opportunities for progress.

As we navigate the complexities of life, optimism reminds us that resilience is not just about enduring—it is about thriving. It empowers us to see beyond immediate difficulties, to trust in our capacity for change, and to inspire those around us with hope and possibility. In the resilient mindset, optimism is not a luxury—it is a necessity, a guiding light that illuminates the path to a stronger, more fulfilled life.

Letting Go of What You Can't Control

Life is filled with uncertainties, setbacks, and outcomes that lie beyond our influence. While it is natural to desire control, clinging to what we cannot change often leads to frustration, anxiety, and a diminished sense of well-being. True resilience comes not from trying to control every aspect of life but from learning to let go of what lies beyond our grasp and focusing instead on what we can influence. This shift in perspective, championed by both ancient philosophy and modern psychology, offers a path to greater peace, clarity, and inner strength.

The Wisdom of Stoic Philosophy

The Stoics, ancient philosophers known for their practical approach to life, emphasized the importance of distinguishing between what we can and cannot control. Epictetus, a former slave turned philosopher, famously taught, "Some things are up to us, and some things are not." According to the Stoics, our thoughts, choices, and actions are within our control, while external events, the opinions of others, and the outcomes of our efforts are not.

This simple yet profound insight forms the foundation of Stoic resilience. By focusing on our own attitudes and actions, we reclaim a sense of agency, even in the face of adversity. At the same time, by accepting the limits of our control, we free ourselves from unnecessary worry and frustration. This dual focus—acting where we can and letting go where we cannot—creates a balance that fosters both serenity and strength.

Consider the example of Marcus Aurelius, the Roman emperor and Stoic philosopher. During his reign, Marcus faced countless challenges, from military conflicts to political intrigue and personal loss. Despite these pressures, his writings in *Meditations* reflect a deep commitment to Stoic principles. Marcus reminded himself to "bear in mind that it is not the external things that disturb us, but our judgment of them." His ability to maintain composure and focus on what he could control—his own character and decisions—enabled him to lead with wisdom and resilience.

The Psychological Perspective on Control

Modern psychology echoes the wisdom of the Stoics, emphasizing the importance of focusing on controllable factors for mental health and resilience. One key concept in this field is the locus of control, which refers to an individual's belief about what influences their life. People with an internal locus of control believe they can shape their circumstances through their actions, while those with an external locus of control feel their lives are determined by external forces.

Research shows that individuals with an internal locus of control tend to be more resilient and proactive in the face of challenges. However, an overly rigid sense of control can lead to burnout and frustration when confronted with the inevitable uncertainties of life. Balancing this perspective with an acceptance of external factors is essential for cultivating resilience.

Another psychological framework, acceptance and commitment therapy (ACT), emphasizes the importance of accepting what cannot be changed while committing to meaningful action. ACT teaches individuals to focus on their values and goals rather than becoming entangled in efforts to control the uncontrollable. This approach aligns closely with Stoic philosophy, offering practical tools for navigating life's uncertainties.

Historical Examples of Letting Go

History is filled with examples of individuals who achieved resilience by letting go of what they could not control and focusing on what they could. One striking example is Abraham Lincoln, whose leadership during the American Civil War was marked by both immense challenges and profound personal losses. Lincoln often faced criticism, setbacks, and uncertainty, yet he remained steadfast in his vision for a united nation.

Lincoln's ability to persevere was rooted in his acceptance of what lay beyond his control — such as the unpredictable outcomes of battles — and his unwavering commitment to what he could influence, including his decisions, policies, and leadership. By focusing on his own efforts and trusting in the broader process, Lincoln exemplified the power of letting go to navigate complex and uncertain times.

Practical Steps for Letting Go

While the concept of letting go is simple, practicing it requires intentional effort and self-awareness. The following strategies can help cultivate this mindset in daily life:

1. **Distinguish Between Influence and Control**: When faced with a challenge, take a moment to identify what aspects of the situation are within your control and what are not. For example, while you cannot control how others behave, you can control your response to their actions.

2. **Practice Acceptance**: Acceptance does not mean resignation or complacency — it means acknowledging reality as it is, without resistance or denial. This mindset creates space for clarity and action. For instance, accepting a delay or setback allows you to focus on adapting rather than dwelling on frustration.

3. **Reframe Setbacks**: Shifting your perspective on setbacks can help you let go of unproductive worries. Instead of seeing a challenge as an obstacle, view it as an opportunity to practice resilience and learn from the experience.

4. **Cultivate Mindfulness**: Mindfulness practices, such as meditation or deep breathing, can help you let go of ruminative thoughts and return to the present moment. By focusing on what is here and now, you can reduce the mental clutter associated with trying to control the uncontrollable.

5. **Focus on Values and Actions**: When external circumstances feel overwhelming, grounding yourself in your core values and taking meaningful action can provide a sense of purpose and direction. For example, if you value kindness,

focus on small acts of compassion even in difficult situations.

The Freedom of Letting Go

Letting go of what we cannot control is not a
surrender—it is a liberation. It frees us from
the mental and emotional burdens of trying to
force outcomes or change things beyond our
influence. This freedom allows us to channel
our energy into what truly matters: our own
attitudes, actions, and growth.

Consider the metaphor of a ship navigating a
storm. The captain cannot control the weather
or the waves, but they can adjust the sails, steer
the rudder, and maintain their focus on the
destination. Similarly, by letting go of the uncontrollable and focusing on our own choices,
we navigate life's uncertainties with greater
confidence and resilience.

A Resilient Mindset for Life

Letting go of what we cannot control is a practice that grows stronger with time and experience. Each time we release the need for control,

we strengthen our ability to accept, adapt, and persevere. This mindset not only enhances our resilience but also deepens our sense of peace and fulfillment.

As we embrace this perspective, we discover that life's uncertainties are not barriers but opportunities to cultivate strength and wisdom. By focusing on what we can control and letting go of the rest, we create space for clarity, growth, and the enduring power of resilience.

Practicing Mental Agility

Life's only constant is change. Whether we face personal transitions, global upheavals, or unexpected challenges, our ability to adapt determines how we navigate uncertainty. Mental agility—the capacity to shift perspectives, embrace new ideas, and respond flexibly to change—is a cornerstone of resilience. It enables us to face adversity with creativity and confidence, transforming obstacles into opportunities for growth.

The Nature of Mental Agility

Mental agility is not about being unfocused or fickle. Rather, it is the ability to maintain clarity while adapting to evolving circumstances. This balance allows us to pivot when necessary without losing sight of our core values and goals. Agility requires openness to new information, the willingness to challenge assumptions, and the courage to change course when the situation demands it.

Consider the story of Charles Darwin, whose theory of evolution revolutionized science. Darwin's intellectual agility was evident in his ability to synthesize observations, challenge established beliefs, and adapt his thinking as new evidence emerged. His work reminds us that resilience is not about rigidity but about the capacity to evolve.

The Role of Perspective in Agility

Mental agility begins with perspective. By adopting a broad, flexible outlook, we can approach challenges with curiosity rather than resistance. This shift in mindset allows us to see possibilities where others see limitations.

The practice of perspective-taking, a key component of mental agility, involves stepping outside our habitual ways of thinking to consider alternative viewpoints. This skill is particularly valuable in conflict resolution, where understanding another person's perspective often leads to creative solutions. For example, leaders who approach disputes with empathy and openness foster collaboration and innovation, transforming challenges into opportunities for progress.

Historical Examples of Agility in Action

Throughout history, individuals and organizations that demonstrated mental agility have achieved remarkable success. One such example is the Apollo 13 mission, famously described as a "successful failure." When an explosion jeopardized the lives of the astronauts aboard, NASA's team had to adapt rapidly, devising innovative solutions to bring the crew safely back to Earth. Their ability to think creatively under pressure and reframe the mission's objectives exemplifies the power of mental agility in overcoming crises.

Another example is the transformation of IBM in the 1990s. Faced with declining relevance in a rapidly changing tech industry, CEO Lou Gerstner led a dramatic pivot from hardware to services and software. This strategic shift required a willingness to question long-held assumptions and embrace new paradigms. IBM's reinvention highlights the importance of agility in navigating complex and uncertain environments.

Philosophical Reflections on Adaptability

Philosophers have long explored the importance of adaptability in navigating life's uncertainties. The Taoist principle of *wu wei*, often translated as "effortless action," emphasizes the value of aligning with the natural flow of circumstances rather than resisting them. This approach encourages us to remain flexible and open, responding to change with grace rather than rigidity.

The Stoics, too, emphasized the importance of adaptability. Marcus Aurelius wrote, "You have power over your mind—not outside events. Realize this, and you will find strength." This perspective reminds us that while external circumstances may be beyond our control, our response to them is always within our power. By cultivating mental agility, we gain the ability to navigate life's challenges with resilience and poise.

Techniques for Cultivating Mental Agility

Building mental agility is an ongoing practice that involves cultivating specific habits and mindsets. One effective technique is cognitive reframing—shifting your interpretation of a situation to uncover opportunities or solutions. For example, instead of viewing a career setback as a failure, you might see it as a chance to explore new directions or develop untapped skills.

Another strategy is fostering a growth mindset, as popularized by psychologist Carol Dweck. A growth mindset involves viewing abilities and intelligence as malleable, which encourages experimentation and learning from mistakes. By embracing the idea that challenges are opportunities for growth, we become more adaptable and resilient.

Mindfulness practices also support mental agility by enhancing awareness and reducing reactivity. Techniques such as meditation or mindful breathing create a pause between stimulus and response, allowing us to approach challenges with greater clarity and flexibility. This practice is particularly valuable in high-pressure situations, where mental agility can make the difference between success and stagnation.

The Value of Experimentation

Mental agility thrives on experimentation — the willingness to try new approaches, take calculated risks, and learn from outcomes. This mindset fosters creativity and resilience, enabling us to adapt to changing circumstances and uncover innovative solutions.

For example, Thomas Edison's invention of the light bulb was the result of thousands of experiments. Rather than seeing failed attempts as setbacks, Edison viewed them as essential steps in the discovery process. His approach exemplifies the value of persistence and flexibility in achieving breakthroughs.

In our own lives, cultivating a spirit of experimentation might involve exploring new hobbies, learning unfamiliar skills, or adopting alternative strategies for solving problems. Each experiment, regardless of its outcome, contributes to our growth and enhances our capacity for adaptation.

Mental Agility in Relationships

Mental agility is equally vital in our interactions with others. Relationships often require flexibility—whether it's adjusting expectations, navigating differences, or responding to changing dynamics. By remaining open to new perspectives and approaches, we strengthen our connections and build resilience in the face of challenges.

For example, a parent navigating a teenager's shifting needs might find that adapting their communication style fosters greater understanding and trust. Similarly, a leader who listens to their team's diverse viewpoints can create a culture of collaboration and innovation.

The Long-Term Benefits of Mental Agility

The rewards of mental agility extend far beyond immediate challenges. Over time, this skill fosters a mindset of adaptability and resilience that enhances every aspect of life. By remaining open to change and willing to grow, we develop the confidence to face uncertainty with optimism and strength.

Mental agility also deepens our sense of purpose and fulfillment. When we approach life with curiosity and flexibility, we engage more fully with our experiences, embracing both the joys and the lessons they offer. This mindset allows us to navigate life's complexities with grace, turning challenges into opportunities for growth and transformation.

Embracing Agility as a Way of Life

Mental agility is not a fixed trait but a dynamic practice—a way of thinking and being that evolves over time. As we cultivate this skill, we discover that life's uncertainties are not threats to be avoided but opportunities to be embraced. By staying open, adaptable, and curious, we unlock the potential to thrive in a world of constant change.

In the resilient mindset, mental agility is more than a tool—it is a way of life. It empowers us to navigate challenges with creativity and confidence, transforming obstacles into stepping stones on the path to growth and fulfillment. Through this practice, we cultivate not only resilience but also the freedom to live authentically and fully, no matter what life brings.

CHAPTER 6: BUILDING EMOTIONAL FORTITUDE – STRENGTH OF THE HEART

Emotional Resilience in History

Emotional resilience—the ability to navigate and recover from life's most profound challenges—has been a defining trait of humanity's greatest leaders, thinkers, and visionaries. While intellectual brilliance and strategic skill are often celebrated, history reveals that emotional strength is equally vital for enduring crises and inspiring others. By examining historical examples of emotional resilience, we can uncover valuable lessons about cultivating inner fortitude in our own lives.

Abraham Lincoln: Resolute in the Face of Tragedy

Abraham Lincoln, often regarded as one of the greatest American presidents, exemplified emotional resilience during some of the nation's darkest hours. Leading a divided country through the Civil War required extraordinary strength—not just in policy but in heart. Lincoln faced immense personal and professional challenges, including the loss of his young son Willie to illness in 1862, a grief that compounded the weight of overseeing a bloody and contentious conflict.

Despite these trials, Lincoln demonstrated an unwavering commitment to his principles and an ability to remain composed under pressure. His resilience was rooted in his capacity for introspection, empathy, and humor, which he often used to diffuse tense situations. Lincoln's ability to weather emotional storms and maintain his vision of a united nation serves as a powerful reminder that emotional strength can sustain both leaders and their causes.

Viktor Frankl: Finding Meaning in Suffering

During World War II, Viktor Frankl, an Austrian psychiatrist and Holocaust survivor, endured unimaginable suffering in Nazi concentration camps. Stripped of his family, possessions, and professional identity, Frankl found solace and strength in his belief that life's meaning could be discovered even in the most harrowing circumstances. His groundbreaking book, *Man's Search for Meaning*, chronicles his experiences and insights, emphasizing the role of emotional resilience in overcoming adversity.

Frankl observed that those who survived the camps often possessed a profound sense of purpose—whether it was the hope of reuniting with loved ones or the determination to complete unfinished work. His philosophy, known as logotherapy, suggests that the search for meaning is central to human resilience. Frankl's story illustrates that emotional fortitude is not about avoiding pain but about finding meaning within it, a lesson that resonates universally.

Mahatma Gandhi: The Power of Nonviolence

Mahatma Gandhi's leadership during India's struggle for independence was marked by extraordinary emotional resilience. As the architect of the nonviolent resistance movement, Gandhi faced imprisonment, physical assaults, and relentless criticism. Despite these hardships, he remained steadfast in his commitment to nonviolence and justice.

Gandhi's emotional strength stemmed from his deep spirituality and unwavering belief in the power of truth (*satyagraha*). He practiced self-discipline and reflection, which enabled him to endure personal suffering without succumbing to bitterness or despair. Gandhi's ability to inspire millions through his resilience underscores the transformative power of emotional strength in achieving collective goals.

Eleanor Roosevelt: Courage in Adversity

Eleanor Roosevelt, one of the most influential First Ladies in American history, overcame significant personal challenges to become a champion of human rights and social justice. Born into a wealthy family, Eleanor faced a series of emotional traumas, including the loss of both parents at a young age and the betrayal of her husband, Franklin D. Roosevelt.

Rather than retreat into bitterness, Eleanor used her experiences to cultivate empathy and strength. She became a tireless advocate for marginalized communities, leveraging her platform to fight for civil rights, women's rights, and global peace. Her emotional resilience was evident in her ability to navigate public life with grace and authenticity, even in the face of criticism. Eleanor's legacy reminds us that emotional strength is not the absence of vulnerability but the ability to transform pain into purpose.

Philosophical Foundations of Emotional Resilience

The emotional resilience demonstrated by these historical figures aligns with philosophical teachings that emphasize the importance of inner strength and perspective. The Stoics, for instance, believed that our emotional responses to external events are within our control. Marcus Aurelius wrote, "You have power over your mind—not outside events. Realize this, and you will find strength." This Stoic principle encourages us to focus on our thoughts and attitudes rather than being overwhelmed by circumstances.

Similarly, Buddhist teachings emphasize the impermanence of emotions and the value of mindfulness in cultivating resilience. By observing emotions without attachment or aversion, we can navigate life's ups and downs with greater equanimity. These philosophical frameworks provide timeless strategies for building emotional fortitude in the face of adversity.

Lessons from History for Modern Challenges

The stories of Lincoln, Frankl, Gandhi, and Roosevelt demonstrate that emotional resilience is not an innate trait but a skill that can be developed through practice and intention. Their experiences highlight several key principles:

1. **Purpose Provides Strength**: Emotional resilience is often fueled by a sense of purpose. Whether it's Lincoln's vision of a united nation or Frankl's search for meaning, purpose gives us the motivation to persevere through difficulties.

2. **Reflection Builds Resilience**: Self-awareness and introspection are essential for managing emotions. Leaders like Gandhi and Roosevelt used reflection to navigate their challenges and maintain their emotional balance.

3. **Empathy Enhances Connection**: Emotional resilience is not about isolation—it is about fostering connections with others. Empathy allows us to build relationships that provide support and inspiration during tough times.

4. **Vulnerability is Not Weakness**: The willingness to acknowledge and confront emotions is

a sign of strength, not weakness. By embracing vulnerability, we create space for growth and healing.

Cultivating Emotional Resilience Today

While the challenges we face may differ from those of historical figures, the principles of emotional resilience remain universal. Cultivating this strength begins with self-compassion — treating ourselves with the same kindness and understanding we would offer to a friend. It also involves developing healthy coping strategies, such as mindfulness practices, journaling, and seeking support from trusted individuals.

Equally important is the ability to find meaning in adversity. Whether through reflection, faith, or service to others, discovering a sense of purpose helps us navigate life's challenges with greater clarity and strength. By embracing these practices, we can build the emotional resilience needed to face modern challenges with courage and grace.

A Legacy of Strength

The emotional resilience demonstrated by history's greatest figures serves as both inspiration and instruction. Their stories remind us that emotional strength is not about avoiding hardship but about rising to meet it with integrity and purpose. As we cultivate our own emotional fortitude, we join a legacy of resilience that transcends time, empowering us to face life's trials with unshakable strength of heart.

The Role of Self-Compassion

In moments of failure, rejection, or hardship, the harshest critic is often the voice within. While self-criticism might seem like a motivator, it frequently exacerbates pain, fuels feelings of inadequacy, and undermines resilience. In contrast, self-compassion—a mindset of kindness and understanding toward oneself—emerges as a powerful tool for emotional fortitude. Far from indulgence or complacency, self-compassion fosters strength, adaptability, and the capacity to bounce back from life's inevitable setbacks.

What Is Self-Compassion?

Self-compassion, as defined by psychologist Dr.

Kristin Neff, involves three key components: self-kindness, recognition of shared humanity, and mindfulness. Self-kindness means treating oneself with care and understanding rather than harsh judgment. Recognition of shared humanity acknowledges that suffering is a universal experience, reminding us that we are not alone in our struggles. Finally, mindfulness encourages us to observe our emotions without becoming overwhelmed or suppressing them.

These elements combine to create a foundation of inner strength. By replacing self-criticism with self-compassion, we cultivate an emotional environment that allows us to process pain, learn from challenges, and move forward with resilience.

The Science Behind Self-Compassion

Research highlights the profound impact of self-compassion on mental health and resilience. Studies show that individuals who practice self-compassion experience lower levels of anxiety, depression, and stress. They are also more likely to persevere in the face of failure, as self-compassion buffers against feelings of shame and inadequacy.

One study, published in the *Journal of Personality and Social Psychology*, found that self-compassionate individuals were more likely to view failure as a learning opportunity rather than a reflection of their worth. This perspective fosters a growth mindset, enabling people to adapt and thrive despite setbacks.

Self-compassion also has physiological benefits. It reduces levels of cortisol, the stress hormone, while increasing oxytocin, the "feel-good" hormone associated with trust and bonding. These hormonal shifts create a sense of calm and connection, reinforcing emotional resilience.

Historical Examples of Self-Compassion

History offers compelling examples of individuals who demonstrated self-compassion in their darkest hours, using it as a source of strength and recovery. One such figure is Nelson Mandela, who spent 27 years in prison during South Africa's apartheid era. Despite the immense hardship, Mandela avoided self-pity or bitterness. Instead, he practiced self-kindness, reflecting on his values and purpose. This inner compassion allowed him to emerge from prison not with vengeance but with a vision of reconciliation and unity, becoming a global symbol of resilience and forgiveness.

Another example is Helen Keller, who faced profound challenges as a deaf-blind individual in a society with limited accommodations. Keller's ability to embrace her humanity and extend kindness to herself in moments of frustration fueled her determination. She once wrote, "Keep your face to the sunshine, and you cannot see a shadow." Her self-compassion enabled her to focus on possibilities rather than limitations, inspiring countless others through her advocacy and writing.

Philosophical Reflections on Self-Compassion

Philosophical traditions across cultures have long emphasized the importance of self-compassion as a cornerstone of resilience. In Buddhism, compassion begins with oneself. The practice of *metta*, or loving-kindness meditation, involves directing warmth and care toward oneself before extending it to others. This inward focus fosters a sense of emotional stability and interconnectedness, which is essential for navigating life's challenges.

The Stoics, too, recognized the value of treating oneself with kindness. While Stoicism often emphasizes discipline and self-control, it also advocates for accepting one's imperfections. Marcus Aurelius wrote, "Don't be ashamed of needing help. You have a duty to fulfill just like a soldier on the wall of battle. So what if you are injured and cannot climb up without another's help?" This acknowledgment of human vulnerability reflects a Stoic form of self-compassion, where acceptance and self-care are seen as integral to resilience.

The Misconceptions About Self-Compassion

A common misconception is that self-compassion leads to complacency or self-indulgence. Critics argue that being kind to oneself might diminish accountability or hinder growth. However, research contradicts this assumption. Self-compassion does not mean avoiding responsibility or ignoring areas for improvement—it means addressing them from a place of understanding rather than harsh judgment.

For example, a student who fails an exam might berate themselves with thoughts of inadequacy, leading to anxiety or avoidance. In contrast, a self-compassionate approach would involve acknowledging the disappointment, recognizing the effort made, and identifying constructive steps for improvement. This mindset encourages both emotional recovery and practical action.

Practical Ways to Cultivate Self-Compassion

Cultivating self-compassion is a practice that involves intentional effort and reflection. One effective technique is the use of compassionate self-talk. When faced with a setback, imagine how you would comfort a friend in a similar situation, and then direct those words toward yourself. This practice helps reframe inner dialogue, replacing criticism with encouragement.

Another powerful tool is journaling. Writing about challenges from a compassionate perspective allows us to process emotions and gain clarity. For instance, reflecting on a difficult experience through the lens of shared humanity—reminding ourselves that others have faced similar struggles—can reduce feelings of isolation and self-blame.

Mindfulness practices also play a crucial role in self-compassion. By observing emotions without judgment, mindfulness creates space for self-kindness to emerge. Techniques such as guided meditations or body scans can help anchor us in the present moment, fostering a sense of calm and acceptance.

The Ripple Effect of Self-Compassion

The benefits of self-compassion extend beyond the individual, influencing relationships and communities. When we treat ourselves with kindness, we are better equipped to extend compassion to others. This ripple effect fosters empathy, cooperation, and resilience in interpersonal dynamics.

For example, a leader who practices self-compassion is more likely to create a supportive and understanding work environment. By modeling self-care and emotional balance, they inspire others to do the same, contributing to a culture of trust and mutual support.

The Freedom of Self-Compassion

At its core, self-compassion is an act of liberation. It frees us from the burden of self-judgment and perfectionism, allowing us to embrace our humanity with grace. This freedom creates a foundation for resilience, enabling us to face challenges with courage and clarity.

As we cultivate self-compassion, we discover that strength does not come from harshness or denial but from understanding and acceptance. By treating ourselves with the kindness we deserve, we unlock the emotional fortitude to navigate life's trials and emerge stronger on the other side. In the journey of resilience, self-compassion is not a detour—it is the way forward.

Managing Emotional Triggers

Emotional triggers are like hidden currents beneath the surface of our lives. They lie dormant until a word, event, or situation activates them, often leading to disproportionate reactions. These triggers can disrupt our emotional balance, cloud our judgment, and strain our relationships if left unchecked. Learning to recognize and manage emotional triggers is a vital step in cultivating emotional resilience and maintaining composure in the face of life's challenges.

Understanding Emotional Triggers

An emotional trigger is any stimulus that evokes a strong emotional reaction, often tied to past experiences or deeply held beliefs. Triggers can vary widely, from a dismissive comment to a specific smell or song, and they are highly personal. For example, someone who experienced childhood criticism may feel disproportionately upset by feedback at work, while another person may feel defensive during discussions about money due to financial struggles in their past.

These reactions are not inherently negative—they often serve as signals that something important to us is being challenged. However, when triggers go unexamined, they can lead to impulsive behavior, miscommunication, and prolonged distress. By understanding and managing these responses, we regain control over our emotions and create space for thoughtful, constructive action.

The Psychology of Triggers

Emotional triggers are deeply rooted in the brain's survival mechanisms, particularly the amygdala, which governs the fight-or-flight response. When the amygdala perceives a threat — whether physical or emotional — it activates a cascade of physiological reactions, including increased heart rate, rapid breathing, and heightened alertness. This response, while useful for immediate danger, can override rational thinking in non-threatening situations, leading to reactive behavior.

Psychologists often refer to this as "amygdala hijacking," where the emotional brain takes over, leaving the rational brain temporarily offline. Managing triggers involves calming the amygdala's response and re-engaging the prefrontal cortex, which governs reasoning and decision-making. This process requires self-awareness, mindfulness, and deliberate practice.

Recognizing Your Triggers

The first step in managing emotional triggers is identifying them. This requires self-reflection and a willingness to explore the origins of strong emotional reactions. Journaling can be a valuable tool in this process, allowing you to document triggering events, your reactions, and the underlying emotions or memories they evoke.

For instance, if a heated argument with a colleague leaves you disproportionately upset, reflecting on the interaction may reveal deeper feelings of inadequacy or fear of rejection. Understanding these underlying emotions helps you separate the trigger from the reaction, enabling you to approach similar situations with greater awareness and composure.

Mindfulness practices, such as meditation or body scans, can also enhance your ability to recognize triggers. By observing your thoughts and physical sensations without judgment, mindfulness creates a pause between stimulus and response, allowing you to choose a more measured reaction.

Strategies for Managing Triggers

Once you've identified your triggers, the next step is developing strategies to manage them effectively. One powerful approach is reframing—shifting your perspective on the triggering event. For example, if a colleague's curt tone triggers feelings of inadequacy, reframing might involve reminding yourself that their behavior reflects their stress level rather than your worth.

Another technique is grounding, which involves using sensory input to anchor yourself in the present moment. This might include taking deep breaths, focusing on the sensation of your feet on the ground, or observing the details of your surroundings. Grounding helps calm the nervous system, reducing the intensity of emotional reactions.

Setting boundaries is also crucial for managing triggers, particularly in relationships or environments that consistently provoke strong emotions. For instance, if family discussions about politics are a recurring source of tension, setting a boundary around these topics can prevent

unnecessary conflict and protect your emotional
well-being.

Historical Examples of Emotional Mastery

Throughout history, individuals who mastered
their emotional triggers have demonstrated extraordinary resilience and leadership. One notable example is Nelson Mandela, who, despite
enduring decades of imprisonment, maintained
composure and grace in the face of provocation.
Mandela's ability to rise above anger and resent-
ment, even toward those who oppressed him,
was a testament to his emotional fortitude. By
reframing his experiences as opportunities for
growth and reflection, he transformed personal
pain into a powerful force for reconciliation.

Another example is Mahatma Gandhi, whose
philosophy of nonviolence required exceptional
emotional discipline. Gandhi often faced hostil-
ity and provocation but refused to react impulsively. Instead, he used moments of tension to
practice patience and self-control, embodying
the principles of his movement. His ability to
manage emotional triggers not only strengthened his resolve but also inspired millions to

follow his example.

The Role of Philosophy in Emotional Management

Philosophical traditions offer valuable insights into managing emotional triggers. The Stoics, for example, emphasized the importance of focusing on what is within our control—our thoughts and actions—while accepting what lies beyond it. Epictetus advised, "It's not what happens to you, but how you react to it that matters." This perspective encourages us to approach triggers as opportunities to practice self-mastery rather than as threats to our equilibrium.

Buddhism similarly teaches the value of non-attachment, recognizing that clinging to expectations or outcomes often exacerbates emotional distress. By cultivating mindfulness and acceptance, we can observe triggers without becoming entangled in their emotional intensity. This practice allows us to respond thoughtfully rather than react impulsively, fostering a sense of inner peace.

Practical Exercises for Trigger Management

Building emotional resilience requires practice. One effective exercise is visualization, where you mentally rehearse responding to a known trigger with composure and confidence. For example, if public speaking triggers anxiety, visualizing yourself speaking calmly and effectively can help desensitize the fear response.

Another exercise is the "STOP" technique: Stop what you're doing, Take a breath, Observe your emotions and surroundings, and Proceed with intention. This simple practice interrupts the automatic response cycle, giving you the space to choose a more thoughtful reaction.

Finally, cultivating gratitude can help shift your focus from triggers to positive aspects of your life. By regularly reflecting on what you're grateful for, you build a foundation of emotional balance that makes it easier to navigate challenges.

Embracing Triggers as Opportunities

Emotional triggers, though often uncomfortable, are not inherently negative. They provide valuable insights into our inner world, highlighting areas for growth and healing. By approaching triggers with curiosity and compassion, we transform them from sources of distress into catalysts for resilience.

As we learn to recognize and manage our triggers, we reclaim our emotional equilibrium and strengthen our capacity to face life's challenges with grace. This practice not only enhances our well-being but also deepens our relationships and empowers us to navigate the complexities of life with confidence and composure. In the journey of emotional resilience, managing triggers is not just a skill—it is a profound act of self-mastery.

Emotional Agility in Action

In the face of life's ever-changing circumstances, emotional agility is the ability to navigate feelings with clarity, flexibility, and intention. Unlike rigidity, which seeks to control or suppress emotions, agility encourages us to move through emotions thoughtfully, learning from them and adapting to their lessons. It is a dynamic skill that fosters resilience, balance, and a deeper connection to ourselves and others. By

putting emotional agility into action, we transform our emotional landscape into a source of
strength and wisdom.

What is Emotional Agility?

Psychologist Susan David, who popularized
the concept of emotional agility, defines it as
the ability to approach emotions with curiosity, acceptance, and courage. It is not about
avoiding negative emotions or forcing positiv-
ity but about recognizing, understanding, and
responding to emotions in ways that align with
our values and goals.

For example, a person experiencing anxiety
before a presentation might acknowledge the
emotion without judgment, identify its root
(fear of failure or desire for approval), and use
it as motivation to prepare more thoroughly.
Emotional agility enables this shift from reactive
to proactive, turning challenging emotions into
opportunities for growth.

The Philosophical Roots of Agility

The concept of emotional agility aligns with

philosophical teachings on mindfulness and adaptability. The Stoics, for instance, emphasized the importance of accepting emotions as natural while maintaining control over our responses. Marcus Aurelius advised, "You have power over your mind—not outside events. Realize this, and you will find strength." This perspective encourages us to engage with emotions without being overwhelmed by them, creating space for thoughtful action.

Buddhist philosophy similarly teaches the value of observing emotions without attachment. By practicing mindfulness, we can acknowledge the impermanence of emotions, recognizing them as passing phenomena rather than fixed states. This awareness fosters agility, allowing us to respond with clarity and compassion rather than being swept away by emotional tides.

Practical Exercises for Emotional Agility

Developing emotional agility requires intentional practice, grounded in both reflection and action. The following exercises offer accessible tools for cultivating this vital skill:

1. Journaling for Clarity

Writing is a powerful tool for processing emotions and gaining insight into their origins. Regular journaling allows us to explore our feelings, identify patterns, and reflect on how emotions influence our thoughts and actions.

For instance, after a challenging day, you might write about the emotions you experienced, what triggered them, and how you responded. This practice not only fosters self-awareness but also helps you identify areas for growth and strategies for future situations.

Journaling can also be structured around specific prompts, such as "What is this emotion teaching me?" or "How can I respond to this situation in a way that aligns with my values?" These prompts encourage curiosity and intentionality, key components of emotional agility.

2. Mindfulness Practices

Mindfulness, the practice of being fully present and aware of the moment, is foundational to emotional agility. By observing emotions without judgment, mindfulness creates space for reflection and choice.

A simple mindfulness exercise is the "RAIN" method:
- **R**ecognize the emotion.
- **A**ccept it without resistance.
- **I**nvestigate its cause and impact.
- **N**urture yourself with compassion and understanding.

For example, if you feel frustration after a difficult conversation, you might recognize the emotion, accept its presence, investigate its connection to unmet expectations, and nurture yourself with a reminder of your capacity for growth. This process transforms frustration into a moment of learning and self-compassion.

3. Reframing Emotional Narratives

Reframing involves shifting the way we interpret and respond to emotions. It is particularly helpful when dealing with negative emotions, as it encourages us to see challenges as opportunities for growth.

Consider the story of Thomas Edison, who famously reframed failure as part of the discovery
process. When asked about his many unsuccess-
ful attempts to create the light bulb, he replied,
"I have not failed. I've just found 10,000 ways
that won't work." Edison's mindset exemplifies emotional agility, turning frustration into
determination.

In practice, reframing might involve asking,
"What can I learn from this emotion?" or "How
can I use this experience to grow?" These questions shift the focus from the discomfort of the
emotion to its potential for transformation.

4. Cultivating Emotional Flexibility

Flexibility is at the heart of emotional agility. It
involves adapting to changing circumstances
without losing sight of your core values. One
way to cultivate flexibility is through role-play-
ing or visualization exercises, which allow you
to explore different perspectives and responses.

For example, if you feel stuck in a conflict, you
might imagine how the situation looks from the
other person's perspective. This exercise not

only fosters empathy but also helps you identify alternative approaches to resolution.

The Ripple Effect of Emotional Agility

Emotional agility is not just a personal practice — it has a profound impact on our relationships and communities. By responding to emotions thoughtfully, we create a ripple effect of understanding and collaboration. For instance, a leader who models emotional agility in the workplace fosters a culture of openness and resilience, empowering their team to navigate challenges with confidence.

On a broader scale, emotional agility enables us to engage with societal issues in meaningful ways. By approaching complex emotions like anger or grief with curiosity and compassion, we transform them into catalysts for action and change. This mindset allows us to contribute to the greater good while maintaining our emotional balance.

Stories of Emotional Agility in Action

Throughout history, individuals who demonstrated emotional agility have left enduring legacies of strength and wisdom. One example is Eleanor Roosevelt, who overcame personal insecurities and public criticism to become a champion of human rights. Her ability to navigate complex emotions with grace and resolve enabled her to advocate for marginalized communities and inspire millions.

Another example is Maya Angelou, whose poetry and activism were shaped by her ability to transform pain into power. Angelou's emotional agility allowed her to confront systemic injustice while maintaining hope and resilience, offering a blueprint for others to do the same.

Embracing Emotional Agility as a Lifelong Practice

Emotional agility is not a destination but a journey—a lifelong practice of engaging with emotions thoughtfully and intentionally. As we cultivate this skill, we discover that emotions, both positive and negative, are not obstacles to be avoided but pathways to greater understanding and growth.

By integrating exercises like journaling, mindfulness, and reframing into our daily lives, we build the capacity to navigate life's complexities with clarity and confidence. In doing so, we not only strengthen our emotional resilience but also create a foundation for meaningful, fulfilling relationships and experiences.

Emotional agility empowers us to face life's challenges with courage and adaptability, turning every twist and turn into an opportunity for growth. It is a skill that transforms not just how we feel but how we live—rooted in authenticity, guided by values, and resilient in the face of change.

CHAPTER 7: COLLECTIVE RESILIENCE – STRENGTH IN COMMUNITY

The Power of Connection

Resilience is often seen as an individual quality, a measure of personal strength and determination. Yet history and science reveal a profound truth: resilience is not cultivated in isolation. It is deeply rooted in connection—the bonds we share with others and the sense of purpose that arises from collective effort. Social connections provide emotional support, foster belonging, and amplify our ability to endure and thrive. The power of connection is both timeless and universal, a cornerstone of human survival and success.

The Role of Connection in Human Evolution

Connection is an intrinsic part of being human. From our earliest days as hunter-gatherers, survival depended on collaboration and community. Small groups worked together to secure food, protect one another from predators, and care for the young and elderly. These bonds were not just practical—they were emotional, creating a sense of safety and belonging that sustained individuals through hardship.

Anthropological studies highlight how social bonds continue to be vital for resilience. In modern times, connection remains one of the most significant predictors of well-being. Psychologist Dr. John Cacioppo, a pioneer in the study of loneliness, found that strong social ties improve physical health, increase longevity, and buffer against the effects of stress. His research underscores the idea that connection is not a luxury but a necessity for thriving in the face of adversity.

Historical Examples of Collective Resilience

The power of connection is vividly illustrated in moments of collective resilience throughout history. One striking example is the solidarity of the British people during World War II. Under the relentless bombing of the Blitz, communities in London and other cities came together to support one another, sharing food, shelter, and encouragement. The resilience of these communities, often described as the "Blitz spirit," became a symbol of hope and defiance against the odds.

Similarly, the American civil rights movement

of the 1960s demonstrated the transformative power of connection and shared purpose. Activists like Martin Luther King Jr. emphasized the importance of unity in the fight for justice. The movement's success was built on the bonds forged among individuals and organizations, creating a collective strength that overcame systemic oppression. The marchers, sit-ins, and freedom riders exemplified how connection fosters courage and resilience, even in the face of immense adversity.

Philosophical Reflections on Connection

Philosophy, too, highlights the importance of connection in building resilience. The African concept of *ubuntu*, often translated as "I am because we are," reflects the belief that our humanity is inextricably linked to the well-being of others. Archbishop Desmond Tutu, a proponent of this philosophy, described it as the recognition that "my humanity is bound up in yours, for we can only be human together." This perspective encourages us to see connection not just as a source of strength but as a moral imperative.

The Stoics also valued connection, emphasizing the interdependence of humanity. Marcus
Aurelius wrote in *Meditations*, "What brings no
benefit to the hive brings none to the bee." This
insight reminds us that our resilience is tied to
the resilience of the communities to which we
belong, reinforcing the idea that we are stronger
together.

Modern Science and the Power of Connection

Modern neuroscience provides further evidence
of the power of connection. The hormone oxytocin, often called the "bonding hormone," is re-
leased during acts of trust, empathy, and affec-
tion. Oxytocin not only strengthens social bonds
but also reduces stress and promotes feelings of
calm and security. This physiological response
highlights the deep connection between emotional resilience and social relationships.

In times of crisis, connection activates neural
pathways associated with hope and problem-solving. Studies on disaster survivors reveal that those who maintain strong social ties
are more likely to recover and rebuild. Connection provides a sense of shared purpose and

mutual support, transforming adversity into an opportunity for growth and collaboration.

Practical Applications of Connection

Building and sustaining meaningful connections is a powerful way to cultivate resilience in everyday life. This begins with small, intentional actions—reaching out to a friend, joining a community group, or simply offering a kind word to someone in need. These moments of connection, though seemingly minor, create ripples that strengthen the fabric of relationships and communities.

For example, workplaces that prioritize connection often see higher levels of resilience among employees. Leaders who foster collaboration, trust, and open communication create environments where individuals feel valued and supported. Similarly, families that cultivate strong bonds through shared activities and honest conversations are better equipped to navigate challenges together.

Another practical application is the practice of gratitude within relationships. Expressing appreciation for others strengthens bonds and reinforces the positive aspects of connection. Whether through a heartfelt thank-you note or a verbal acknowledgment, gratitude deepens relationships and enhances mutual resilience.

The Ripple Effect of Connection

The impact of connection extends beyond the individual, creating a ripple effect that benefits entire communities. When individuals come together with a shared purpose, their collective strength becomes greater than the sum of its parts. This phenomenon is evident in grass-roots movements, where ordinary people unite to address social, environmental, or political challenges.

One powerful example is the global response to the COVID-19 pandemic. Despite physical dis-tancing, communities found innovative ways to stay connected and support one another, from organizing food drives to cheering for health-care workers. These acts of solidarity not only provided practical assistance but also fostered a sense of hope and togetherness that sustained people through uncertainty.

Strengthening Resilience Through Connection

The power of connection lies not just in its ability to provide comfort but also in its capacity to inspire action. By building relationships rooted in trust, empathy, and shared purpose, we create a foundation for resilience that endures even in the face of adversity.

As we cultivate connection in our lives, we discover that resilience is not a solitary journey—it is a collective endeavor. By leaning on one another, we amplify our strength, find courage in companionship, and create a legacy of hope and resilience for generations to come.

Learning from Collective Struggles

In the face of crisis, the resilience of a community often determines whether it succumbs to adversity or emerges stronger. Throughout history, collective struggles have tested humanity's resolve, showcasing the extraordinary capacity of people to unite, adapt, and rebuild. From revolutions to natural disasters, these moments illuminate the power of shared purpose and

collaboration, offering valuable lessons for navigating challenges in our own lives.

The French Revolution: Unity Against Oppression

The French Revolution, which began in 1789,
stands as a testament to the power of collective
struggle. Faced with widespread poverty, in-
equality, and political corruption, ordinary citizens rose against the monarchy and aristocra-
cy, demanding liberty, equality, and fraternity.
While the revolution was marked by upheaval
and violence, it also demonstrated the strength
of a united population.

At the heart of the revolution was the belief
that collective action could transform society.
Communities organized assemblies, shared resources, and supported one another in the face
of oppression. This unity gave the movement
its momentum, ultimately leading to the aboli-
tion of feudal privileges and the declaration of
human rights.

The French Revolution reminds us that resilience
is not just an individual endeavor—it is a shared

commitment to a better future. It highlights the importance of solidarity in overcoming systemic challenges, a lesson that resonates in contemporary struggles for justice and equality.

The Great Depression: Resilience Through Cooperation

The Great Depression of the 1930s plunged millions into unemployment and poverty, testing the resilience of communities worldwide. In the United States, the crisis gave rise to innovative forms of collaboration and mutual aid. Communities established cooperatives, where members pooled resources to buy food and supplies at reduced costs. Local groups organized "barn raisings" and other collective efforts, helping families rebuild homes and farms.

One of the most enduring legacies of this era is the New Deal, a series of government programs aimed at providing relief and recovery. These initiatives, including public works projects and social security, were shaped by the collective voice of citizens advocating for systemic change. The Great Depression underscores the power of unity and collaboration in rebuilding after

a crisis, demonstrating that shared efforts can
create lasting solutions.

Natural Disasters: The Strength of Togetherness

Natural disasters, though devastating, often
bring out the best in human connection. In the
aftermath of hurricanes, earthquakes, and tsunamis, communities around the world have
demonstrated remarkable resilience through
unity.

One notable example is the response to Hurricane Katrina in 2005. While the initial disaster exposed significant gaps in governmental
preparedness, it also highlighted the strength
of grassroots efforts. Volunteers from across
the country mobilized to provide aid, rebuild
homes, and support displaced families. Faith-based organizations, nonprofits, and neighborhood groups played a crucial role in helping
communities recover.

Similarly, the 2011 earthquake and tsunami
in Japan showcased the resilience of a nation
united by shared purpose. Known as *kizuna*—a

Japanese term for "bond" or "connection" —this spirit of solidarity was evident in the widespread acts of kindness and cooperation. Neighbors shared food and water, businesses offered free services, and volunteers worked tirelessly to rebuild devastated areas. These stories remind us that even in the face of overwhelming loss, collective resilience can bring hope and renewal.

Philosophical Reflections on Collective Struggles

The lessons from collective struggles align with philosophical teachings on the value of unity and mutual support. The African philosophy of *ubuntu*, which emphasizes interconnectedness, teaches that "I am because we are." This worldview underscores the idea that our well-being is intrinsically tied to the well-being of others, encouraging us to act with empathy and collaboration.

The Stoics, too, recognized the importance of community in cultivating resilience. Seneca wrote, "No one can live happily who has regard for himself alone and transforms everything

into a question of his own utility." This perspective highlights the role of connection in fostering
resilience, reminding us that we are stronger
when we stand together.

Lessons for Modern Crises

The lessons of history and philosophy resonate
powerfully in today's world, where collective
struggles continue to shape our lives. From the
global response to climate change to the challenges of the COVID-19 pandemic, these crises
remind us that resilience requires not just individual strength but collective action.

For example, the pandemic underscored the importance of healthcare workers, delivery drivers,
and other essential personnel who kept society
functioning under extraordinary circumstances.
It also highlighted the role of mutual aid networks, where neighbors supported one another
by delivering groceries, providing childcare,
and offering emotional support. These acts of
solidarity demonstrated that resilience is not
about standing alone—it is about standing together.

Similarly, the fight against climate change depends on collective action. Movements like Fridays for Future, led by young activists such as Greta Thunberg, illustrate how unity can amplify voices and inspire systemic change. These efforts remind us that resilience in the face of global challenges requires a shared commitment to sustainability and justice.

Cultivating Resilience Through Unity

Building collective resilience begins with fostering a sense of connection and shared purpose. This involves creating spaces where people can come together, share ideas, and collaborate on solutions. It also requires recognizing and valuing diverse perspectives, as unity is strengthened by inclusivity.

One practical approach is to participate in community initiatives, whether through volunteering, joining local organizations, or supporting grassroots movements. These efforts not only address immediate needs but also build the social bonds that sustain resilience over time.

Another strategy is to engage in dialogue about

shared challenges. By listening to others' experiences and perspectives, we deepen our understanding of the collective struggle and identify opportunities for collaboration. This practice fosters empathy and trust, essential components of collective resilience.

The Legacy of Collective Struggles

The stories of communities overcoming crises through unity and collaboration are more than historical anecdotes—they are enduring lessons about the strength of the human spirit. They remind us that resilience is not an isolated act but a shared journey, one that draws on the power of connection, empathy, and purpose.

As we face the challenges of our time, we can draw inspiration from these examples, knowing that together, we are capable of extraordinary resilience. By learning from collective struggles, we not only honor the past but also create a future defined by hope, solidarity, and strength.

Building a Support Network

In the journey of life, resilience often stems from

the relationships we cultivate. A strong support network acts as a buffer against adversity, providing emotional comfort, practical assistance, and a sense of belonging. Building such a network is not about amassing connections but fostering meaningful relationships rooted in trust, empathy, and mutual support. This section explores the principles and practices for creating and sustaining a network that nurtures resilience and shared strength.

The Value of a Support Network

A support network is more than a collection of individuals—it is a dynamic ecosystem where mutual care and encouragement flourish. Research highlights the profound impact of social support on resilience. Studies show that people with strong networks recover more quickly from setbacks, experience lower levels of stress, and enjoy better physical and mental health.

The benefits of a support network are particularly evident in times of crisis. During natural disasters, pandemics, or personal struggles, those with close-knit relationships are better equipped to cope and rebuild. These connections provide not only practical help—such as sharing resources or offering childcare—but also emotional stability, which is essential for navigating uncertainty.

The Foundations of a Strong Network

Building a support network begins with authenticity and intentionality. The most resilient networks are formed not through convenience or obligation but through shared values, experiences, and mutual respect. These relationships are characterized by:

1. **Trust**: A strong network is built on trust, where individuals feel safe sharing vulnerabilities and seeking help without fear of judgment or betrayal.

2. **Empathy**: Understanding and compassion are cornerstones of supportive relationships. Empathy fosters deeper connections and creates an environment where individuals feel truly heard.

3. **Reciprocity**: A resilient network thrives on give-and-take. Offering support to others not

only strengthens bonds but also reinforces the idea that resilience is a shared endeavor.

Practical Steps to Cultivate a Support Network

While building a network may seem daunting, it begins with small, intentional actions. One of the most effective ways to foster connections is by reaching out—whether to friends, family, colleagues, or community members. A simple act, such as expressing interest in someone's life or offering a listening ear, can lay the foundation for a meaningful relationship.

For instance, joining community organizations or interest groups provides opportunities to connect with like-minded individuals. Shared activities, such as volunteering, attending workshops, or participating in sports, create natural avenues for forming bonds. These environments encourage collaboration and mutual support, strengthening the fabric of the network.

Another strategy is to nurture existing relationships by investing time and effort. Regular check-ins, thoughtful gestures, and shared experiences deepen connections and reinforce the sense of belonging. In the digital age, staying connected has never been easier, with video calls, messaging apps, and social media offering tools to bridge physical distances.

Learning from Historical Examples

History offers inspiring examples of how support networks have fostered resilience in the face of adversity. One such example is the Underground Railroad, a clandestine network of individuals who helped enslaved people escape to freedom in the 19th century. This extraordinary system relied on trust, cooperation, and shared purpose, demonstrating the power of collective effort in overcoming systemic oppression.

Similarly, the Women's Suffrage Movement in the early 20th century highlighted the importance of solidarity. Suffragists across the globe formed alliances, organized campaigns, and supported one another in the fight for equal rights. Their resilience, bolstered by a strong support network, ultimately led to transformative social change.

The Role of Philosophy in Relationships

Philosophical teachings underscore the importance of relationships in cultivating resilience. The concept of *philia*, or brotherly love, was central to ancient Greek philosophy, emphasizing the value of friendships based on mutual respect and shared goals. Aristotle considered such friendships essential for living a virtuous and fulfilling life, describing them as "a single soul dwelling in two bodies."

The Stoics, too, recognized the significance of community in navigating life's challenges. Marcus Aurelius wrote, "We are made for cooperation, like feet, like hands, like eyelids, like the rows of the upper and lower teeth. To act against one another is contrary to nature." This perspective reminds us that humans are inherently interconnected, and our resilience is strengthened through collaboration and mutual support.

Overcoming Challenges in Building Networks

While the benefits of a support network are clear, building one is not without challenges. Barriers such as shyness, past disappointments, or fear of vulnerability can hinder efforts to connect with others. Overcoming these obstacles requires self-awareness and courage.

For instance, practicing vulnerability is a powerful way to deepen relationships. Sharing personal experiences and emotions, even in small doses, fosters trust and encourages others to reciprocate. Similarly, cultivating patience is essential, as meaningful relationships take time to develop.

It is also important to recognize and address toxic relationships that drain energy or undermine resilience. While it may be difficult, setting boundaries or distancing oneself from harmful influences is a necessary step in fostering a supportive network.

The Ripple Effect of a Support Network

A strong support network not only benefits the individuals within it but also creates a ripple effect that strengthens communities. When people feel supported, they are more likely to offer support to others, creating a culture of care and collaboration. This collective resilience has the potential to address broader challenges, from social inequalities to environmental crises.

For example, neighborhood watch programs and community gardens are initiatives born from the strength of support networks. These efforts not only address immediate needs but also build trust and solidarity, contributing to the resilience of the entire community.

Building Resilience Through Relationships

At its core, building a support network is about creating a web of relationships that sustain and uplift us through life's challenges. It is an investment in mutual strength, where the bonds we form become a source of comfort, guidance, and inspiration.

As we cultivate these connections, we discover that resilience is not a solitary endeavor but a shared journey. By reaching out, offering support, and embracing the power of community, we create a foundation for enduring strength and fulfillment. In the face of adversity, it is the ties that bind us that carry us forward, reminding us that we are never truly alone.

Giving and Receiving Support

At the heart of collective resilience lies a profound yet simple truth: we are stronger together. Offering and accepting help, though seemingly opposite acts, are two sides of the same coin. Together, they form the foundation of mutual aid, a dynamic process that sustains individuals and communities through adversity. Understanding the interplay between giving and receiving support not only strengthens our bonds but also deepens our capacity for resilience and compassion.

The Strength in Offering Support

When we extend support to others, we reinforce the very fabric of community. Acts of kindness — whether lending an ear, providing resources, or offering encouragement — foster trust and solidarity. These gestures remind us that resilience is not a solitary endeavor but a shared journey.

One compelling example is the spontaneous networks of aid that emerge in the wake of natural disasters. After the 2010 earthquake in Haiti, grassroots efforts played a critical role in providing food, shelter, and medical care to those affected. Local and international volunteers worked tirelessly to support survivors, demonstrating the power of collective action. These efforts not only alleviated immediate suffering but also inspired hope and unity, proving that even in the darkest moments, the act of giving can light the way forward.

Offering support also enhances the giver's resilience. Research in positive psychology shows that helping others triggers the release of endorphins, creating a phenomenon known as the "helper's high." This physiological response reduces stress, boosts mood, and reinforces a sense of purpose. By focusing on others' needs, we gain perspective on our own challenges, finding strength and fulfillment in the act of service.

The Courage to Receive Support

While offering help may come naturally to many, accepting it can feel uncomfortable or even counterintuitive. Cultural narratives often

celebrate independence and self-reliance, leading individuals to perceive receiving help as
a sign of weakness. Yet the truth is quite the
opposite: allowing others to support us requires
courage, humility, and trust.

Accepting help strengthens relationships by fostering vulnerability and mutual understanding.
When we share our struggles and invite others
to assist us, we create opportunities for deeper
connection. This dynamic is vividly illustrated
in the mentorships and partnerships that have
shaped history. For example, the collaboration
between Mahatma Gandhi and his close confi-
dants during India's independence movement
exemplified the power of reciprocal support.
Gandhi's willingness to rely on others for guidance, strategy, and encouragement was instru-
mental in sustaining the movement's resilience.

Philosophical traditions also highlight the importance of receiving support. The Stoics, for
instance, viewed interdependence as a natural
aspect of human life. Seneca wrote, "What for-
tune has made yours is not your own." This
perspective encourages us to view help not as
charity but as an exchange that strengthens

the bonds of community. Similarly, Buddhist teachings emphasize the interconnectedness of all beings, reminding us that accepting support allows others to practice compassion and generosity.

The Balance Between Giving and Receiving

Resilience is nurtured when giving and receiving support exist in harmony. A community thrives not when a few individuals bear the burden of care but when everyone participates in the mutual exchange of strength. This balance ensures that no one is overwhelmed and that everyone has the opportunity to contribute.

One way to achieve this balance is by practicing self-awareness and open communication. For example, consider a team working on a demanding project. If one member is struggling silently while others overextend themselves to pick up the slack, the imbalance can lead to burnout and frustration. However, when team members communicate openly about their capacities and needs, they can distribute responsibilities more equitably, fostering a supportive environment.

The concept of reciprocity also plays a central role in balancing giving and receiving. In her book *Braiding Sweetgrass*, Robin Wall Kimmerer describes reciprocity as a principle of balance and gratitude, rooted in Indigenous teachings. She writes, "All flourishing is mutual." This philosophy reminds us that both giving and receiving are acts of participation in a shared ecosystem of care, whether in nature or in human relationships.

Overcoming Barriers to Support

Despite the benefits of mutual aid, barriers such as pride, fear of judgment, or a lack of trust can hinder the exchange of support. Overcoming these obstacles begins with fostering a culture of empathy and understanding. By normalizing vulnerability and celebrating acts of both giving and receiving, we create spaces where support is not only accepted but embraced.

For instance, leaders who model vulnerability by sharing their own challenges can inspire others to seek help without fear of stigma. In organizations, initiatives such as peer mentoring or employee assistance programs encourage a culture of mutual support, reinforcing the idea that seeking help is a strength, not a weakness.

On an individual level, practicing gratitude can help dissolve barriers to receiving support. When we view help as a gift rather than an obligation, we are more likely to accept it with grace and appreciation. This mindset shifts the focus from perceived inadequacy to the shared value of connection.

The Ripple Effect of Mutual Aid

When giving and receiving support become integral to a community's fabric, the effects ripple outward, creating a culture of resilience and generosity. This dynamic is evident in movements such as mutual aid societies, which have long served as lifelines for marginalized communities. These organizations, built on principles of solidarity and shared responsibility, provide resources, advocacy, and emotional support to those in need.

A modern example is the global response to the refugee crisis. Grassroots networks of volunteers, nonprofits, and host communities have worked together to offer shelter, education, and opportunities to displaced individuals. This collective effort demonstrates the transformative power of mutual aid, turning compassion into tangible action.

Embracing Mutual Strength

The dynamic of giving and receiving support is a cornerstone of collective resilience. By offering help, we contribute to a culture of care and strengthen our own sense of purpose. By accepting help, we deepen connections and create opportunities for others to practice compassion. Together, these acts form a cycle of mutual strength that sustains individuals and communities through life's challenges.

As we embrace the balance of giving and receiving, we discover that resilience is not about standing alone but about standing together. In the rhythm of mutual aid, we find not only the support we need but also the strength to support others, creating a legacy of hope and solidarity for generations to come.

CHAPTER 8: THE ENDURING SPIRIT – LESSONS FOR A LIFETIME

Integrating Timeless Lessons

As we near the end of this journey through resilience and inner strength, it is essential to reflect on the lessons woven into the pages of this book. These insights, drawn from history, philosophy, and modern science, are not distant ideals but practical tools to be integrated into the rhythms of daily life. By embracing these lessons, we can cultivate a life marked by balance, purpose, and the enduring spirit needed to face life's complexities.

Resilience as a Foundation

At its core, resilience is not merely the capacity to withstand adversity but the ability to grow through it. From the first chapter to this final reflection, the themes of resilience have emerged as both timeless and universal. The stories of individuals like Abraham Lincoln, Viktor Frankl, and Eleanor Roosevelt remind us that resilience is built through self-awareness, a commitment to values, and a willingness to adapt.

Integrating resilience begins with acknowledging that life's challenges are inevitable. Rather than fearing hardship, we can approach it as an opportunity for growth. For instance, when faced with a setback, pause to reflect on the underlying lesson. Ask yourself: "What can this teach me about my strengths, my values, or the areas where I need to grow?" This shift in perspective transforms challenges from obstacles into stepping stones, helping to reinforce resilience in even the most difficult moments.

Inner Strength: A Cultivated Practice

Inner strength, as explored throughout this book, is not an inherent trait but a cultivated practice. It is the result of intentional efforts to align thoughts, emotions, and actions with our deepest values. Historical examples such as Mahatma Gandhi's nonviolent resistance and Marcus Aurelius' Stoic reflections reveal that inner strength arises when we consistently act with integrity and purpose.

To integrate this lesson into daily life, begin by identifying your core values. These are the principles that anchor you, guiding your decisions and actions. Once identified, reflect on how your daily habits and choices align—or conflict—with these values. For example, if one of your core values is compassion, consider how you interact with others during stressful situations. Are you patient and understanding, or do you let frustration dictate your responses? By aligning your actions with your values, you strengthen the foundation of your character, ensuring that your inner strength becomes a reliable guide in all circumstances.

Connection as a Source of Strength

Throughout this journey, the importance of connection has emerged as a recurring theme. From the bonds that sustain us during personal struggles to the collective resilience of communities, our relationships are vital to our strength and well-being. The concept of *ubuntu*—"I am because we are"—captures the essence of this truth. We are not isolated beings but deeply interconnected, and our resilience is amplified through the support, wisdom, and kindness of others.

To integrate this lesson, prioritize the relationships that matter most to you. Make time to nurture meaningful connections, whether through regular conversations, shared activities, or small acts of kindness. At the same time, be open to receiving support. Accepting help is not a sign of weakness but an acknowledgment of our shared humanity. When we allow others to support us, we create opportunities for deeper connection and mutual growth.

The Role of Perspective

One of the most profound lessons explored in this book is the power of perspective. The ability to reframe challenges, embrace patience, and adapt to changing circumstances transforms how we experience life. Viktor Frankl's philosophy of finding meaning in suffering demonstrates that perspective is often the difference between despair and resilience.

Integrating this lesson begins with cultivating mindfulness. When confronted with a challenging situation, take a moment to observe your thoughts and emotions without judgment. Ask yourself: "How am I interpreting this situation? Is there another way to view it that aligns with my goals or values?" For example, a professional setback might initially feel like a failure, but reframing it as an opportunity to learn and grow can shift the experience from frustration to motivation. This practice of perspective-taking is a powerful tool for building emotional resilience and maintaining balance.

Embracing Growth Through Reflection

Throughout history, individuals who have embodied resilience and inner strength have shared a common practice: reflection. From journaling to meditation, these moments of introspection provide clarity, foster growth, and deepen our understanding of ourselves. Reflection is not a passive act but an active process of examining our experiences, identifying lessons, and applying them to future actions.

To incorporate reflection into your life, set aside time each day or week to pause and evaluate your experiences. Consider questions such as: "What challenges did I face, and how did I respond? What strengths did I draw upon, and where can I improve?" Writing these reflections in a journal can be especially powerful, as it allows you to track your growth over time. By engaging in regular reflection, you strengthen your ability to navigate life's complexities with wisdom and intentionality.

Living Resiliently: A Holistic Approach

The lessons of resilience and inner strength are not isolated practices but interconnected principles that shape how we live, work, and relate to others. Integrating these lessons requires a holistic approach that encompasses mind, body, and spirit. For example:

- **Mind**: Cultivate emotional agility and mental flexibility, embracing change and uncertainty with curiosity and courage.

- **Body**: Support your resilience through healthy habits, such as regular exercise, adequate sleep, and mindful eating. These practices enhance your physical energy, which is essential for emotional and mental resilience.

- **Spirit**: Align your actions with your purpose, drawing inspiration from the values and beliefs that matter most to you.

By attending to each of these dimensions, you

create a life that is not only resilient but also rich with meaning and fulfillment.

The Enduring Nature of These Lessons

As we integrate these timeless lessons into our lives, it is important to remember that resilience and inner strength are not destinations but ongoing pursuits. There will be moments of success and moments of struggle, yet each step along the journey deepens our understanding and fortifies our character.

This book's teachings, drawn from history, philosophy, and personal stories, are guides for navigating the ever-changing landscape of life. They remind us that even in the face of uncertainty, we possess the tools to endure, grow, and thrive. By embracing these lessons and applying them with intention, we can build lives marked by resilience, inner strength, and a profound sense of purpose.

In the end, the enduring spirit is not about being unshaken by life's challenges—it is about rising to meet them, again and again, with courage, wisdom, and heart.

A Lifelong Journey of Growth

Resilience and inner strength are not destinations but processes—ongoing journeys that evolve with the seasons of life. They are dynamic, requiring us to adapt, grow, and recommit to the principles that sustain us. By embracing this perspective, we free ourselves from the illusion of perfection and recognize that strength is built incrementally, through both triumphs and trials.

Resilience as a Process, Not a Trait

Many view resilience as an innate characteristic—something we either possess or lack. Yet research and lived experience reveal a different truth: resilience is cultivated over time. Like a muscle, it grows stronger with practice, challenge, and deliberate effort.

Consider the story of Nelson Mandela, who endured 27 years of imprisonment during apartheid in South Africa. Mandela's resilience was not a fixed trait but a process he nurtured daily. Through self-reflection, discipline, and a commitment to his values, he transformed his suffering into a source of strength. Mandela's life reminds us that resilience is not a static quality but a practice that evolves as we confront life's challenges.

To see resilience as a journey is to accept that setbacks are not failures but opportunities for growth. Each obstacle we face adds to our reservoir of strength, teaching us lessons that prepare us for the future. This perspective shifts the focus from achieving a fixed state of resilience to embracing the ongoing work of becoming resilient.

The Role of Growth Mindset

A growth mindset—the belief that abilities and traits can be developed through effort and learning—is central to viewing resilience and inner strength as lifelong pursuits. Psychologist Carol Dweck, who coined the term, emphasizes that a growth mindset fosters perseverance, adaptability, and a willingness to take risks.

For example, a person with a growth mindset might approach a professional setback not as a reflection of their inadequacy but as an opportunity to learn and improve. This perspective allows them to reframe failure as part of the journey, rather than as an endpoint. By adopting a growth mindset, we create the conditions for continuous development, enabling resilience and inner strength to flourish over time.

Learning from Life's Seasons

Life unfolds in seasons, each bringing its own challenges and opportunities for growth. The resilience we need as young adults forging careers and relationships differs from the resilience required in later years, as we navigate losses, transitions, and legacies. Recognizing these shifts allows us to adapt our approach, drawing on the lessons of the past while remaining open to new ways of being.

The philosopher Friedrich Nietzsche captured this idea with his famous words: "That which does not kill us makes us stronger." While resilience is not about seeking hardship, it is about finding meaning and strength in the experiences that shape us. By reflecting on the lessons of each season, we gain the wisdom to face the next with greater clarity and resolve.

For instance, a young parent navigating sleepless nights and the demands of raising a child might draw resilience from the support of family and the knowledge that this phase is temporary. Years later, as an empty nester adjusting to a quieter home, they might find strength in rediscovering personal passions and building new relationships. Each season of life offers unique opportunities to grow, reminding us that resilience is a dynamic and evolving quality.

Historical Examples of Lifelong Growth

History is replete with examples of individuals who viewed resilience and inner strength as lifelong pursuits. One such figure is Helen Keller, who overcame the challenges of being deaf and blind to become a renowned author and activist. Keller's journey of growth did not end with her initial achievements; she continued to advocate for social justice throughout her life, demonstrating that resilience is not a one-time act but an enduring process.

Another example is Maya Angelou, whose life was marked by continuous reinvention and resilience. From overcoming childhood trauma to becoming a celebrated poet, writer, and civil rights activist, Angelou embraced growth as a lifelong journey. Her ability to transform pain into power serves as a testament to the enduring nature of resilience.

Practical Ways to Embrace Lifelong Growth

To integrate the idea of resilience as a journey into daily life, it is helpful to adopt practices that support ongoing growth and adaptation. One such practice is self-reflection. By regularly examining our thoughts, actions, and experiences, we gain insight into how we respond to challenges and where we can grow. Journaling, meditation, or simply setting aside time for introspection can help anchor this practice.

Another approach is to seek out new challenges. Resilience grows not in comfort but in the face of uncertainty and change. By stepping outside our comfort zones—whether by learning a new skill, taking on a difficult project, or pursuing a long-held dream—we build the capacity to navigate future challenges with confidence.

Mentorship is also a powerful tool for lifelong growth. Learning from those who have walked similar paths provides guidance and inspiration, while mentoring others reinforces our own resilience. This reciprocal relationship creates a cycle of growth that benefits both the mentor and the mentee.

Philosophical Reflections on Growth

Philosophical traditions offer profound insights into the nature of growth and resilience. The Stoics, for example, emphasized the importance of cultivating *areté*, or excellence, through continuous effort. Seneca wrote, "As long as you live, keep learning how to live." This perspective encourages us to approach life as a classroom, where each experience offers a lesson.

Buddhism similarly teaches the concept of impermanence, reminding us that growth is a constant process. By embracing change and remaining open to new experiences, we align ourselves with the natural flow of life, fostering resilience and inner strength.

The Beauty of the Journey

Viewing resilience and inner strength as lifelong pursuits frees us from the pressure of perfection. It allows us to celebrate progress rather than fixate on outcomes, finding joy in the process of becoming. This perspective encourages us to approach each day with curiosity and a willingness to grow, knowing that every step—no matter how small—contributes to our resilience.

As we journey through life, we will inevitably encounter moments of doubt, fear, and struggle. Yet these moments are not the end of the story; they are the chapters where our character is forged. By embracing resilience as a journey, we transform challenges into opportunities for growth, discovering new depths of strength within ourselves.

Ultimately, the lifelong pursuit of resilience and inner strength is not about reaching a final destination but about walking the path with intention, courage, and grace. It is a journey that enriches our lives and inspires those who walk alongside us, reminding us that growth is not just possible—it is inevitable.

Adapting to New Challenges

Life is marked by change, often sudden and unforeseen. Whether it's a career shift, a global crisis, or a personal loss, challenges frequently arise that test our resilience and adaptability. While uncertainty can feel daunting, it also offers opportunities for growth and transformation. The principles of resilience and inner strength provide a framework for navigating these moments, equipping us to face new challenges with clarity and confidence.

The Nature of Unforeseen Challenges

Unforeseen challenges disrupt our sense of stability and force us to confront the unknown. These moments often feel overwhelming because they challenge the structures and routines we rely on for security. However, history and psychology reveal that adaptability—the ability to adjust our mindset, behaviors, and strategies—is key to thriving in uncertain times.

For instance, the COVID-19 pandemic upended lives across the globe, forcing individuals, businesses, and communities to adapt rapidly.

Teachers shifted to online classrooms, health-care workers redefined protocols, and families found creative ways to stay connected despite physical distancing. These adaptations, though challenging, exemplify the resilience required to navigate unprecedented circumstances.

Historical Lessons in Adaptability

History offers countless examples of individuals and communities who have demonstrated remarkable adaptability in the face of adversity. One striking example is the Apollo 13 mission in 1970. When an oxygen tank exploded aboard the spacecraft, the lives of the astronauts were at risk, and the mission's original objectives became impossible. Faced with this crisis, NASA engineers and the crew worked together to devise innovative solutions, using limited resources to ensure the astronauts' safe return. This story highlights the importance of flexibility, creativity, and teamwork in overcoming new challenges.

Similarly, Harriet Tubman's efforts in leading enslaved individuals to freedom through the Underground Railroad required constant adaptation. Tubman's ability to navigate shifting threats and circumstances, while maintaining her commitment to a higher purpose, underscores the role of adaptability in building resilience. Her story reminds us that resilience is not about rigidly adhering to a plan but about responding to change with courage and ingenuity.

The Role of Mindset in Adaptation

Our ability to adapt begins with our mindset. Psychologist Carol Dweck's concept of a growth mindset is particularly relevant here. By viewing challenges as opportunities to learn and grow, we shift from a state of fear and resistance to one of curiosity and possibility. This perspective allows us to approach new circumstances with openness, reducing the stress and anxiety often associated with change.

For example, consider someone facing an unexpected job loss. A fixed mindset might lead them to focus on the loss and view it as a personal failure. In contrast, a growth mindset enables them to see the situation as an opportunity to explore new career paths, develop new skills, or pursue long-held passions. This shift in perspective not only eases the emotional toll of change but also empowers individuals to take proactive steps forward.

Practical Strategies for Adapting to New Challenges

While mindset is foundational, effective adaptation also requires actionable strategies. The following practices can help individuals navigate unforeseen challenges with resilience and strength:

1. Embrace Flexibility

Rigid thinking often exacerbates the stress of change. Flexibility involves being willing to adjust goals, expectations, and strategies as circumstances evolve. This might mean exploring alternative paths to achieve a desired outcome or redefining success in light of new realities.

2. Focus on Controllables

As emphasized in Stoic philosophy, directing energy toward what we can control—and letting go of what we cannot—is essential for maintaining balance. In the face of uncertainty, focusing on small, manageable actions creates a sense of agency and forward momentum.

3. Seek Support

Resilience is not a solitary pursuit. Reaching out to trusted friends, family, or mentors for advice and encouragement strengthens our capacity to adapt. Collective problem-solving often yields insights and solutions that might not emerge in isolation.

4. Cultivate Patience

Adaptation takes time. By practicing patience and giving ourselves grace during periods of adjustment, we create the space needed to learn and grow. This aligns with the teachings of mindfulness, which emphasize staying present and accepting each moment as it comes.

Philosophical Reflections on Adaptability

Philosophy offers profound insights into the art of adaptation. The Stoics, for example, taught that external events are beyond our control, but our responses to them are within our power. Epictetus wrote, "It's not what happens to you, but how you react to it that matters." This perspective encourages us to focus on our internal resilience rather than external circumstances.

Buddhist philosophy similarly emphasizes impermanence, reminding us that change is a natural part of life. By embracing impermanence, we free ourselves from attachment to specific outcomes, allowing us to flow with life's transitions rather than resist them.

Modern Applications of Adaptability

In today's fast-paced world, adaptability is more important than ever. Technological advancements, economic shifts, and global challenges demand that individuals and organizations remain flexible and innovative. Leaders who cultivate adaptability within themselves and their teams create environments where resilience thrives.

One notable example is the evolution of the technology industry. Companies like IBM and Microsoft have demonstrated the ability to reinvent themselves in response to changing markets, transitioning from hardware-focused businesses to leaders in software and cloud services. Their success underscores the importance of adaptability as a driver of long-term resilience.

The Rewards of Adaptation

Adapting to new challenges not only helps us navigate the immediate situation but also fosters personal growth and confidence. Each time we successfully adapt, we expand our capacity to handle future uncertainties. This cumulative effect creates a foundation of resilience that serves us throughout life.

Moreover, adaptation often leads to unexpected opportunities. What begins as a disruption can become a catalyst for positive change, opening doors to new experiences, relationships, and achievements. By remaining open to these possibilities, we transform challenges into stepping stones toward a richer, more fulfilling life.

A Commitment to Growth

Adaptation is not a one-time act but an ongoing

practice. As life continues to evolve, so too must our strategies for resilience. By committing to a mindset of growth and embracing the principles outlined in this book, we equip ourselves to face whatever comes our way.

Ultimately, the ability to adapt is a testament to the enduring spirit of humanity. It reflects our capacity to learn, grow, and thrive in the face of uncertainty. By applying these principles to new and unforeseen challenges, we not only build resilience but also create lives filled with purpose, strength, and possibility.

Living with Purpose and Strength

Resilience and inner strength find their highest expression when paired with purpose. To live a life grounded in meaning is to navigate challenges with clarity and direction, drawing strength from a vision that transcends immediate circumstances. Purpose imbues our actions with significance, anchoring us in the face of uncertainty and propelling us toward fulfillment.

The Transformative Power of Purpose

Purpose is not a destination but a guiding force—a compass that aligns our decisions and efforts with our core values and aspirations. Throughout history, individuals who have lived with purpose have demonstrated extraordinary resilience, channeling their inner strength to overcome immense obstacles.

One powerful example is Malala Yousafzai, who, despite surviving a near-fatal attack for advocating girls' education, remained steadfast in her mission. Malala's unwavering commitment to her purpose not only sustained her through personal adversity but also inspired a global movement for educational equity. Her story exemplifies how purpose transforms challenges into opportunities for impact, enabling individuals to endure and thrive.

Similarly, Nelson Mandela's journey reflects the profound interplay between purpose and resilience. Imprisoned for 27 years during South Africa's apartheid era, Mandela maintained hope and dignity by holding fast to his vision of justice and equality. His ability to endure hardship and emerge as a unifying leader underscores the strength that purpose can provide in the most trying circumstances.

Defining Your Purpose

Living with purpose begins with introspection. What drives you? What values and causes resonate deeply with your sense of identity? Purpose is not limited to grand ambitions; it can be found in the quiet dedication to family, the pursuit of personal growth, or the desire to contribute meaningfully to your community.

To uncover your purpose, reflect on moments when you felt most alive and aligned with your values. These moments often reveal the essence of what matters most to you. For instance, a person who feels fulfilled while mentoring others might find purpose in guiding and empowering the next generation.

Purpose is also shaped by the intersection of passion, skills, and the needs of the world. This concept, often referred to as *ikigai* in Japanese philosophy, invites us to explore how our unique abilities can address meaningful challenges. By aligning our strengths with a greater cause, we create a sense of purpose that is both personal and impactful.

The Relationship Between Purpose and Resilience

Purpose acts as an anchor during life's storms. When faced with setbacks, having a clear sense of why we persevere provides motivation and focus. Viktor Frankl, a Holocaust survivor and renowned psychiatrist, captured this dynamic in his book *Man's Search for Meaning*. Frankl observed that individuals who found meaning in their suffering were more likely to endure it. He famously wrote, "He who has a why to live can bear almost any how."

This principle applies to challenges both great and small. A person striving to recover from a health setback might find strength in their purpose to care for loved ones or pursue cherished dreams. Similarly, someone navigating a career transition may draw resilience from their commitment to personal growth or societal contribution. Purpose reframes adversity as a stepping stone rather than a stumbling block, enabling us to face challenges with determination and grace.

Purpose as a Source of Fulfillment

Beyond resilience, purpose is a wellspring of joy and fulfillment. When our actions align with our deeper values, we experience a sense of coherence and satisfaction that enriches every aspect of life. This alignment fosters not only personal well-being but also a positive ripple effect on those around us.

Consider the example of educators who dedicate themselves to shaping young minds. Their work often involves long hours and numerous challenges, yet their purpose—the belief in the transformative power of education—sustains them. This sense of meaning not only energizes their efforts but also inspires their students, creating a cycle of impact that extends far beyond the classroom.

Cultivating Strength Through Purpose

Living with purpose requires not only identifying what matters most but also committing to it with intention and action. This commitment often demands courage, as purpose-driven paths are rarely free of obstacles. Yet it is through these challenges that we cultivate inner strength, deepening our resilience and capacity for growth.

Practical steps to strengthen your commitment to purpose include:

- **Set Intentional Goals**: Define specific, actionable steps that align with your purpose. These goals provide direction and a sense of progress, reinforcing your connection to what matters most.

- **Celebrate Small Wins**: Acknowledge and appreciate the milestones along your journey. Each achievement, no matter how small, is a testament to your dedication and resilience.

- **Surround Yourself with Support**: Engage with individuals who share or support your purpose. These connections offer encouragement, accountability, and inspiration, fostering a sense of community and shared strength.

Philosophical Reflections on Living with Purpose

Philosophy offers timeless wisdom on the role of purpose in leading a meaningful life. Aristotle's concept of *eudaimonia*, often translated as "flourishing," emphasizes living in alignment with one's virtues and fulfilling one's potential. According to Aristotle, true happiness arises not from fleeting pleasures but from a life dedicated to meaningful pursuits.

Similarly, the Stoics viewed purpose as essential for resilience. Marcus Aurelius wrote, "What we do now echoes in eternity." This perspective encourages us to act with intention, knowing that our efforts contribute to a legacy of purpose and impact.

The Legacy of Purposeful Living

Living with purpose and strength creates a legacy that extends beyond our individual lives. It inspires others to pursue their own meaningful paths, contributing to a culture of resilience and shared humanity. The examples of leaders, activists, and ordinary individuals who have lived purposefully remind us that our actions, however small, have the power to shape the world.

As we embrace purpose in our own lives, we discover that it is not a burden but a gift—a source of strength, fulfillment, and connection. It empowers us to face challenges with courage, navigate change with clarity, and leave a lasting impact on those we encounter.

A Life of Purpose and Strength

In the end, living with purpose is not about perfection or grand achievements. It is about showing up each day with intention, aligning our actions with our values, and finding meaning in the journey. This approach transforms resilience and inner strength from abstract concepts into lived experiences, enriching our lives and inspiring others along the way.

As we close this exploration of enduring wisdom, let us carry forward the principles of resilience, inner strength, and purpose. By doing so, we create lives not only marked by perseverance but also filled with meaning, joy, and the enduring spirit of humanity.

CONCLUSION: THE JOURNEY FORWARD

Resilience is a journey—a lifelong pursuit that shapes who we are and how we navigate the complexities of life. As we reach the conclusion of this book, it is worth pausing to reflect on the enduring wisdom we've explored together. From the stories of remarkable individuals to the timeless teachings of philosophy and the actionable insights of modern science, we've delved into what it means to cultivate inner strength and persevere through life's challenges.

Yet the true value of these lessons lies not in their theoretical richness but in their practical application. Resilience, inner strength, and purpose are not abstract ideals reserved for extraordinary circumstances; they are skills and perspectives that can be integrated into our daily lives, offering clarity, balance, and fulfillment.

This book was not merely a collection of ideas but an invitation—a call to embrace resilience as a dynamic process, to cultivate inner strength through intentional practice, and to live a life imbued with purpose and meaning. As we part ways, let us revisit these themes one last time, weaving them together into a vision for the journey ahead.

Resilience: Rising to Life's Challenges

Life is unpredictable, often challenging us in ways we never anticipated. Resilience is the thread that connects our ability to endure, adapt, and ultimately thrive in the face of adversity. It is not about avoiding hardship but learning to grow through it, transforming challenges into opportunities for growth.

Through the stories of historical figures like Viktor Frankl, Nelson Mandela, and Malala Yousafzai, we've seen resilience in action. Their lives remind us that resilience is not a fixed trait but a practice—a commitment to facing life's difficulties with courage, clarity, and hope.

Resilience begins with a mindset shift. It requires us to view setbacks not as insurmountable barriers but as stepping stones on the path of growth. This perspective empowers us to navigate challenges with determination, recognizing that each obstacle is an opportunity to strengthen our character and deepen our understanding of ourselves.

Inner Strength: Anchoring Ourselves in Values

Inner strength is the foundation of resilience—a wellspring of stability and courage that anchors us during life's storms. It is cultivated through intentional alignment with our core values, enabling us to act with integrity and purpose, even in the most challenging circumstances.

Throughout this book, we've explored how individuals like Marcus Aurelius and Eleanor Roosevelt embodied inner strength, drawing on their values to guide their actions and decisions. Their examples remind us that inner strength is not about unyielding toughness but about staying true to what matters most.

To cultivate inner strength, we must first identify our values and allow them to shape our lives. This requires self-reflection and the courage to live authentically, even when faced with external pressures or uncertainty. When our actions align with our values, we create a sense of co-herence and fulfillment that sustains us through life's challenges.

Purpose: The Guiding Light

Purpose transforms resilience and inner strength from reactive tools into proactive forces for growth and fulfillment. It provides the "why" that sustains us through hardship and moti-vates us to strive for something greater. Purpose is not a destination but a direction—a guiding light that illuminates our path and infuses our actions with meaning.

The examples of individuals like Helen Keller and Mahatma Gandhi highlight the transforma-tive power of purpose. Their lives were marked not by the absence of struggle but by their abili-ty to channel their efforts toward a greater cause. Purpose allowed them to transcend their cir-cumstances and leave a lasting impact on the world.

As we navigate our own journeys, finding and living with purpose becomes a vital part of re-silience. Purpose is not always grand or universal—it can be found in the quiet dedication to nurturing relationships, contributing to our communities, or pursuing personal growth. By aligning our actions with our purpose, we create lives that are not only resilient but also deeply fulfilling.

The Role of Connection

While resilience and inner strength are often seen as individual qualities, they are also profoundly relational. Our connections with others—friends, family, mentors, and communities—serve as sources of strength, inspiration, and support. As the African philosophy of *ubuntu* teaches us, "I am because we are." Our resilience is intertwined with the resilience of those around us.

The stories of collective resilience, from the Underground Railroad to the Great Depression, remind us of the power of unity and shared purpose. These examples highlight the importance of nurturing relationships, offering support, and being open to receiving it. Together, we are stronger than we could ever be alone.

In our own lives, cultivating meaningful connections requires intention and vulnerability. By investing in our relationships and participating in communities, we create networks of support that sustain us through life's challenges. These connections not only strengthen our resilience but also enrich our lives with a sense of belonging and shared humanity.

Adapting to the Unknown

Change is a constant, and the ability to adapt is a hallmark of resilience. Whether facing personal transitions, societal shifts, or global challenges, our willingness to embrace uncertainty and learn from it determines our capacity to thrive.

Adaptability requires both flexibility and focus. It involves letting go of what we cannot control and directing our energy toward what we can. The principles of Stoic philosophy and mindfulness, explored in this book, offer practical tools for cultivating this mindset. By staying present and responding thoughtfully to change, we transform uncertainty into an opportunity for growth.

A Call to Action

As you close this book and step back into the rhythm of daily life, the real work begins. The lessons we've explored together are not meant to remain on these pages—they are meant to be lived. Resilience, inner strength, and purpose are not destinations to be reached but practices to be embraced, day by day, moment by moment.

Start small. Reflect on the lessons that resonate most deeply with you and consider how they might shape your actions and choices. Whether it's cultivating patience, embracing vulnerability, or aligning your actions with your values, each step you take brings you closer to a life marked by resilience and fulfillment.

Remember, this journey is not about perfection but about progress. There will be moments of doubt, setbacks, and uncertainty, but these are not signs of failure—they are opportunities to grow stronger. Trust in the process and in your capacity to rise.

The Legacy of Resilience

The enduring spirit of resilience and inner strength is not just about surviving—it's about thriving. It's about facing life's challenges with courage, navigating its complexities with wisdom, and finding meaning in its uncertainties. By embracing these principles, you not only enrich your own life but also inspire those around you, creating a ripple effect of strength and hope.

This book is not the end of your journey—it is the beginning. As you move forward, carry these lessons with you, and let them guide you in creating a life that reflects your highest values and aspirations. Together, we can build a world where resilience, purpose, and strength are not just ideals but lived realities.

The journey is yours to continue. Go forth with courage, live with intention, and let your enduring spirit shine.

ACKNOWLEDGEMENT

Creating this book has been a journey shaped by the wisdom, encouragement, and support of many remarkable individuals. To all who have walked this path with me, I owe a debt of gratitude.

First and foremost, I extend my heartfelt thanks to the thinkers, philosophers, and historical figures whose lives and ideas inspired these pages. Their resilience, courage, and insights continue to illuminate the human experience.

To my family and friends, thank you for your unwavering belief in me. Your encouragement and understanding have been the foundation of my efforts, reminding me that resilience is best nurtured in the company of those who care.

To my readers, thank you for embracing this book and its message. Your curiosity, reflection, and commitment to growth are what bring these words to life.

Finally, to the unseen hands who contributed to the creation of this work—editors, designers, and mentors—your dedication and expertise have made this book possible. I am deeply grateful for your guidance and collaboration.

This book is a testament to the enduring spirit of resilience, a collective effort born of inspiration and shared purpose. Thank you all for being part of this journey.

ABOUT THE AUTHOR

Felix Grayson's journey into timeless wisdom began in childhood, captivated by the stories of philosophers, leaders, and visionaries who shaped the way we think and live. Growing up in a home filled with books, he spent countless hours exploring ideas that asked life's biggest questions—a curiosity that would later define his work.

After facing his own modern challenges—balancing ambition, uncertainty, and the search for meaning—Felix discovered that the wisdom of the past offers profound guidance for the present. This realization became the foundation for the *Stoned Philosopher* series: a collection dedicated to translating ancient insights into practical lessons for today's world.

Felix's writing is more than reflection—it's an invitation to dialogue with history's greatest minds. Through each book, he helps readers find clarity, resilience, and purpose in their own lives—one timeless idea at a time.

When not writing, Felix enjoys quiet contemplation, deep conversation, and exploring the endless pursuit of wisdom in everyday moments.

www.ingramcontent.com/pod-product-compliance
Lightning Source LLC
Chambersburg PA
CBHW021222130626
46554CB00004B/1325